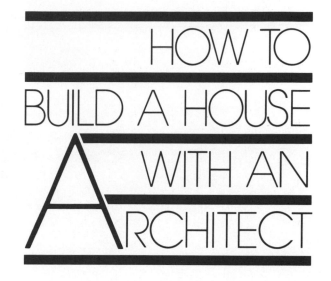

HOW TO BUILD A HOUSE WITH AN ARCHITECT

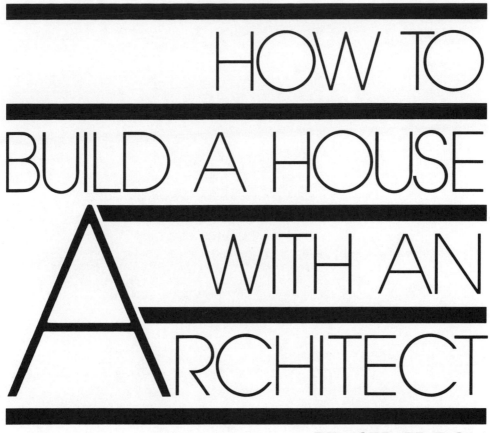

HOW TO BUILD A HOUSE WITH AN ARCHITECT

REVISED EDITION

John Milnes Baker, A.I.A.

PERENNIAL LIBRARY

Harper & Row, Publishers, New York
Cambridge, Philadelphia, San Francisco
London, Mexico City, São Paulo, Singapore, Sydney

Copyright acknowledgments begin on page 223.

ACKNOWLEDGMENTS

Thanks to Kathy Banks for her patience and care in editing and to the Meredith Corporation for making photographs from *Better Homes and Gardens* publications available to me. Also to Bonnie Maharam for running almost all of the *Better Homes and Gardens* photographic sessions. And many thanks to my wife, Liddy, for her considered judgment and advice the innumerable times I asked for her opinion.

First PERENNIAL LIBRARY edition published 1988.

Library of Congress Cataloging-in-Publication Data

Baker, John Milnes, birth date.
  How to build a house with an architect.

  Bibliography: p.
  1. Architectural, Domestic—Handbooks, manuals, etc. 2. Architectural practice—Handbooks, manuals, etc. I. Title.
NA7115.B28   1988   728.3   79-203
ISBN 0-06-055120-8
ISBN 0-06-096251-8 (pbk.)   88 89 90 91 92   10 9 8 7 6 5 4 3 2 1
                                     88 89 90 91 92   10 9 8 7 6 5 4 3 2 1

To my wife, Liddy; my children,
Ian, Jennifer, Jamie, and Hayden,
and my first grandchild,
Florian Dotti

CONTENTS

The house of moderate cost is not only America's major architectural problem but the problem most difficult for her major architects.

Frank Lloyd Wright
The Natural House

PREFACE

Building a house with an architect should be fun. The experience should be one of the most exciting and creative efforts in one's entire life. It can only be so, however, if the client and the architect enjoy that special rapport that comes from an understanding and appreciation of one another's respective roles. The more a client understands the architectural process, the more compatible the partners in this cooperative effort become and the more gratifying the results.

In my own practice I am constantly reminded how little the average client knows about the whole process of building a house and what to expect from his architect at each successive stage.

A couple of years ago some friends were moving to a distant state where they intended to build a house. They asked me how to find the right architect and what to expect from him once they had done so. Because I am an architect myself, I had never before been confronted with this problem, and I found the query rather intriguing. I soon discovered there was no up-to-date, comprehensive book that adequately outlined the process of building a house with an architect, giving suitable illustrative examples of the various phases of the work.

There was clearly a need for a handbook on "how to build a house with an architect," and this book is my response to this need. The accompanying illustrations show examples of such things as "partis," "schematics," "developed design drawings," and "working drawings." Equally important, I have tried to clarify many of the deceptively simple phrases which appear in the American Institute of Architects' "Standard Form of Agreement between Owner and Architect." This contract (A.I.A. Document B141 or B151) governs the architect's entire relationship with his client, and the client should be familiar with it. To help the client understand the document, however, further elaboration of the clauses is necessary.

Architects usually brief their clients in considerable detail at an early stage about the architectural process, covering what happens when and who does what. I have repeated my standard "lecture" innumerable times to my own clients and have found that many of the all-too-familiar misunderstandings that seem to haunt the architectural profession can best be avoided by better communication. There should be a complete step-by-step explanation of the whole process. Most disagreements between architects and clients arise from the client's ignorance of the standard process of planning, designing, and constructing a house—procedures that are far more esoteric to the client than the architect generally realizes. This situation is compounded by the architect's failure to recognize the breakdown in communications that results when he uses professional jargon. Terms like *soffit, plate height, cats,* and *rake* have no meaning to the typical client, and *change orders, field orders,* and *shop drawings* can have misleading connotations.

Another problem arises from the prevalent image of the architect as invariably extravagant and impractical—a myth unfortunately perpetuated by isolated examples. Some clients, however, are literally disappointed if their own experience does not reinforce the image. I am convinced that in certain instances the client wants a house to cost more than he feels justified in spending. If the architect can be blamed for the excessive cost, the owner is relieved of the responsibility for his own extravagance. Sometimes the client offers the rationalization that a third bathroom, for instance, is required for resale value or that the heated garage will cost more if built later. He is right, of course, but good-bye budget! An architect has a responsibility both to himself and to his client to hold the scope of the project in line with the budget without offering any false hopes or promises.

Cost overruns are more often the result of client changes or misunderstandings than of the artistic extravagance of the architect, and they can best be avoided if the client, the architect, and the builder work closely together.

Unfortunately for the client and the profession, an architect does occasionally exhibit a careless disregard for his client's best interests and lets his own egotistical aspirations influence his judgment. The more a client knows what to expect, the more he will get in return. A secure and competent architect need not feel threatened by a client's familiarity with the architect's responsibilities.

It is not my intention to persuade everyone reading this book to go out and build a house. Nor is it my desire to produce a complete treatise on residential design. Rather, my aim is to help anyone undertaking to build a house avoid the typical problems and misunderstandings that so often seem to arise. I will try to clarify the various steps involved and to offer illustrated examples which demonstrate the entire procedure from beginning to end.

In addition to explaining the process itself, I will present some guidelines for judging not only the architectural merits of the completed house, but also the architect's performance over the entire building process. In selecting an architect for your own project, I suggest that you talk to some of his clients and look carefully at his work to determine how successfully he interpreted his other clients' aims and tastes.

I hope that after reading this book your future evaluation of houses will be made with greater understanding of the principles involved. Judgment of any house designed by an architect, or of an alteration, for that matter, should be objective and critical rather than subjective and sentimental, as is so often the case. If you understand the basic principles, your own house-building project will be more stimulating to your architect and the end result will be yours as much as his. If the builder feels the same way, the ideal relationship is achieved.

It has always pleased me that the word *harmony* is derived from the Greek carpenter's term meaning "joinery," or things meshing neatly together. My hope for this book is that it will contribute to the creation of harmonious houses, not only in terms of craftsmanship, but also in the cooperative teamwork of the client, the architect, and the builder.

JOHN MILNES BAKER

Katonah, New York

INTRODUCTION

Whether you decide to buy a ready-built house—new or old—or to build from scratch may depend not only on objective circumstances but also on a sense of purpose in life, an awareness and responsiveness to your surroundings, and your life-style. If you do decide to build, imagination, self-confidence, and vision—as well as a good sense of humor—are far more important characteristics than the size of your pocketbook.

A young bachelor once approached me at a party, saying he would like to build a house but had a very tight budget. How much would I charge and what could I do to help him? I told him that the standard fee for residential work was around 15 percent of the cost of construction. He gulped and quickly decided he couldn't afford what he saw as a substantial extra.

A couple of months went by and he called me up. He wanted to know if I would be willing to look at a proposal he had gotten from a builder who was a self-styled designer.

"Sure," I said, "come on over."

What I saw was a "Cape Cod" with a lifted dormer, housing a living room/dining room, kitchen, two bedrooms, small study, 1½ baths, and carport—all for $18,500. (This was a few years ago!) There was a semblance of a cathedral ceiling in the living room, but the house had terrible circulation problems, boxy rooms, no regard for view or orientation, and was totally devoid of any style, proportion, or character.

I saw what he was after and could not resist the game of one-upmanship. Professional pride, I guess. I suggested a basic scheme and made a few sketches. He was very pleased with my solution and said it was just what he had in mind all along, but immediately he assumed it would cost too much.

The house I designed was less complicated than his original proposal and actually cost less. He hired me on a time basis, and my

BETTER HOMES AND GARDENS CALLED THIS HOUSE THEIR
"FLEXIBLE ALL-TIME FAVORITE"

In 1970 Better Homes and Gardens *selected eighteen houses from across the country as "Designs for the seventies." This modest house for a single man or woman was one of them. In their 1978 fall Building Ideas, the magazine acknowledged this design as their "reader favorite" and described it as "one of the most universally accepted houses* [they] *ever featured."*

Joseph Stakes House
John Milnes Baker, Architect

2ND FLOOR

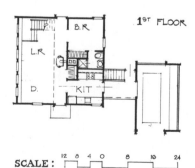

1ST FLOOR

SCALE:

fee was only $1,500. The basic house cost $15,000 with a garage, and he spent $1,000 more on his own. His total outlay was $17,500. He not only saved $1,000 on the original proposal, but the house was written up in a magazine and received national recognition, which increased its resale value substantially. The owner subsequently refused offers of more than double his initial investment and has become one of the profession's best spokesmen, telling people they can't afford to build *without* an architect.

Though this case is an isolated one and no responsible architect would ever claim that employing him will save his client money, he *can* claim to assure him better value for money spent. The architect-designed house need not be expensive, nor the architect's fee a significant consideration. Anyone who can afford to buy a single-family house can afford to build (see pages 207–208).

For some reason that has never been clear to me, however, people will make hundreds of compromises when buying a house but are reluctant to give up anything at all when they build. Even if you can't afford the ultimate dream house, why not explore the possibility of building something the right architect can design in the light of your list of priorities?

When you are searching for a new home the first decision which has to be made is whether to buy an existing house or to build a new one. Buying a house is a lot easier than building from scratch, and far fewer decisions have to be made. You can see what you are getting right from the start and can resign yourself to the house's limitations. If no alterations are required, the cost of an existing house will be fairly clear-cut. This is always reassuring. Also, you are secure in the knowledge that the new house is suited to your tastes and expectations, and represents no threat to your life-style, beliefs, or fundamental principles. Most comforting of all, perhaps, are the flattering assurances of the real-estate broker that your final choice is just the right house for you.

With a ready-built house there is no need to cope with an arrogant and presumptuous stranger who invades the privacy of your comfortable domestic world and challenges you to reevaluate many of your comfortable old beliefs, no need to ask yourself embarrassing and soul-searching questions, such as who you are, where you are going, and what you really expect from life. This disruptive process of self-assessment can easily be avoided by buying a house as you buy a car, a lawn mower, or a TV. But life has far more to offer: the creation of your personal environment could well be one of the most exciting, creative, and stimulating experiences you will ever have in your entire life.

Of course, even if you do decide to build, you need not go to an architect. There are other options, but the results are usually not as satisfactory:

Prefabricated Houses. Since the number of prefabricated designs is so limited, the reason people presumably choose to buy a "prefab" is to save money. There are far fewer savings, however, than most people realize, and compromises are made in the designs to facilitate easier marketing, production, and transportation. Since prefabs are, by definition, built from stock plans, the following paragraph also applies.

Stock Plans. The best stock plans rarely fill all of an individual family's unique requirements, and they cannot possibly take full advantage of a site. The plans of some well-designed houses are usually available for purchase for around $200. If you do decide to use stock plans, you should not attempt to make modifications and you must be very careful how you site the house on your lot with regard to view and orientation.

Designing Your Own House. The main drawback to designing a house for oneself is the inability of most people to judge their own work dispassionately. This is a tremendous liability to any designer, and even some professionals find it a problem. Another disadvantage is that the cost of building a house designed without a knowledge of building techniques and construction methods is apt to be extremely high. Problems during construction are increased because details were not studied thoroughly at the design stage, and the scope of the work usually was not clearly defined in advance.

A common misconception is that builders design houses, but they do not; they copy plans and imitate forms. They simply do not think in abstract terms. This is not a value judgment; it is a simple fact, and no good builder would really attempt to do the architect's job with all it entails. Even an accomplished concert pianist does not have to be a composer or an arranger. They simply do different things.

If you want to build from scratch, or remodel, and none of these options meet your needs, you will have to determine if you need an architect. If you want more out of a house than is generally available in the ready-built market, if you want your own unique personality expressed architecturally in space and form, in mass and texture, and if you need the help of a professional adviser who can help you achieve these goals, then you need an architect.

From the beginning the architect can be helpful to you in many ways. When it comes to selecting a site, for instance, he can point out both potential problems and intrinsic merits that may not be apparent to you and may matter little to the real-estate broker. If you are considering buying an old house and remodeling, the architect can help determine if your family's needs would be met better by buying a lower-priced house and investing more money in fixing it up, rather than spending most of your budget on a higher-priced house, leaving you without sufficient funds to make necessary alterations. The occasional white elephant may be bought at a bargain price because its potential was never appreciated.

The architect plans a house around a family's needs and asks provocative questions to help determine what is really important to the family. When people move they will often discard a piece of furniture they have used out of habit. An architect forces clients to re-evaluate life-style and attitudes; some are discarded, like the old bureau, others are strengthened with the renewed conviction that comes from the knowledge that a system of beliefs has been thoroughly analyzed and consciously chosen rather than simply acquired haphazardly.

One of the chief functions of an architect is to focus on the natural amenities and features of a given site while minimizing the drawbacks. He considers the whole site, its environment and setting, in relation to the unique needs of one particular family.

I had occasion to do half a dozen houses in a summer beach community a few years ago. Several people were surprised to learn I had done them all, because the houses "didn't look anything alike." Of course they didn't—they had been designed for different families with different needs and for different sites, each with its own set of problems and features. As each house was a satisfactory solution to the particular problems of its owner, I liked all of them and considered them "mine."

1. FERENBACH

SIX BEACH HOUSES
BY THE AUTHOR

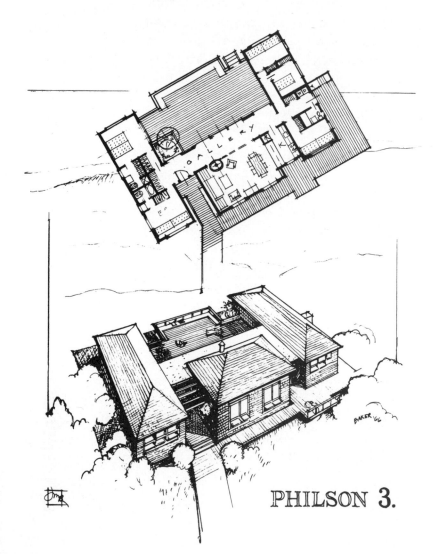

GALLERY

PHILSON **3.**

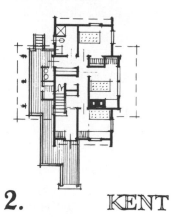

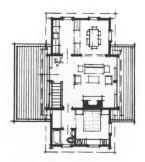

2. KENT

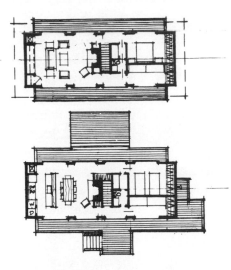

4. SCHOULER

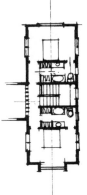

REICH

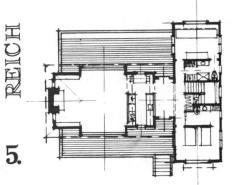

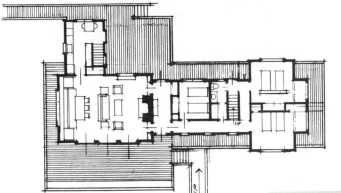

5.

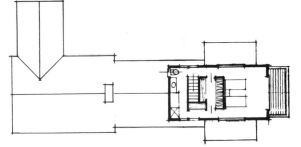

RAMP UP

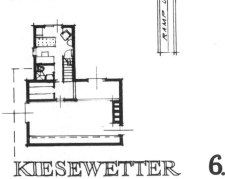

KIESEWETTER 6.

Any architect would have respected the same set of standards. Another architect's houses would certainly not have looked like mine, but neither would they have looked like one another anymore than mine did, unless the architect subscribed to a doctrinaire sect of stylistic imitators.

If you do decide you need an architect, the next step is to find the right one. You should talk to several architects in your area. Steer clear of those who don't design houses as a major part of their work, and be very wary of the inexperienced student and the unlicensed "designer."

Architects should be much more than clever draftsmen with a flair for design. They are licensed by each state for the protection of "life, health, and the public welfare." Their training is much broader than most people realize, and in many instances involves four years of graduate school. By law, in most states, this must be followed by a minimum of three years' apprenticeship in a licensed architect's office before becoming eligible even to sit for the seven licensing exams.

These exams cover the gamut of the profession—site planning, design (a twelve-hour exam in itself), structural engineering, mechanical systems (including heating, ventilation, and air conditioning), construction techniques, history of architecture, and professional practice. Though an architect may very well rely on consultants for engineering problems, both mechanical and structural, he has to have a thorough understanding of the basic engineering principles. He must also be a realistic businessman and have a sound understanding of the law as it relates to his particular field.

Residential work is generally considered by the profession to be the most demanding branch of architecture. It is not a particularly lucrative field for the architect, who also must often spend time with clients at odd hours, at their convenience in the evenings and on weekends. If an architect does this kind of work, he does it because he loves it and because of the rewards and satisfaction apart from the fee.

An architect is a professional adviser who can, and often does, act as his client's agent. He should be chosen on the basis of his competence, integrity, and discretion, and you, the client, should have complete confidence in the architect's ability to interpret and serve your best interests in all facets of the building operation. In addition to his professional qualifications, the architect chosen should also be someone you like and find personally compatible.

If you can't find the right architect locally, go farther afield. A radius of 150 miles is not unrealistic. Ask to see an architect's work and talk to his former clients. Don't make a negative judgment on an isolated case, as personalities may clash, emotions run high; even a careful and experienced professional can have a problem with an occasional job. But a pattern will emerge, and you should find an architect who stands out as someone you can work with.

Larger firms whose members generally specialize in one or two particular aspects of a project literally cannot afford to do a single-family house, where personal involvement with the client should be sustained throughout the entire building process. In residential work there are many details that must be remembered from one phase to another and which cannot possibly be conveyed to an assistant or a partner, no matter how thoroughly he is briefed.

When talking to an architect initially, don't worry that you're going to "get married" right away. You have an "engagement period" during which you discuss your goals and the possible means of attaining them, and determine fairly quickly if there is a genuine rapport between you. If you are not confident that a particular architect really understands your problems and goals, it is better to terminate the relationship. (This works both ways!) Discuss the possibility with your architect at the first meeting and have a clear understanding what your financial commitment is if you should go your separate ways.

In each section of the text I indicate what percentage of the architect's total services has been completed by the end of the phase under consideration and the appropriate fee for that particular service. In the appendix the subject of fees and the architect's compensation are discussed at length.

I will have accomplished my purpose if this book succeeds in making your relationship with your architect and the entire process of building your house an enjoyable and stimulating experience.

Unless your motives for wanting an architect-designed house are well-defined and meaningful to your family, you diminish your chances of getting a house that is genuinely gratifying to you or your architect. For it is a fact that most architects believe they do their best work for clients who know what they want and understand the complex process they are letting themselves in for.

William Houseman
House and Garden *(August 1966)*

1 THE PROBLEM
The Program—The Owner's Domain

The process of building a house with an architect is divided into three phases: program, design, and construction. Another way of putting it is, perhaps: the problem, the solution, and the implementation. Though all three phases overlap to some extent, the first is essentially determined by the owner, the second by the architect, and the third by the builder.

There are actually two parts to the program. The first is sometimes called the functional program, and the second the architectural program.

FUNCTIONAL PROGRAM

This is essentially a written description of the owner's needs, wishes, and priorities. It describes the character and use of every room in the house and analyzes the individual space requirements of each member of the family.

When developing a functional program, most architects will encourage their clients to produce magazine clippings, sketches, rough floor plans, and so on, with a running commentary about each item. All of these furnish clues which the architect can interpret, and by asking the right questions, he can establish a hierarchy of priorities in case budget considerations preclude inclusion of each and every idea. Dislikes will also emerge, some rational, others based only on prejudice. For example, a client may have an aversion to aluminum glass sliding doors, having seen them only in motels. When shown what they look like with rocks and shrubbery, his entire visual concept might be completely revised.

The architect uses his interpretive ability to define the essential nature of the problem, so that the design process, the solution, can be based on the client's realistic personal needs and desires rather than on some momentary whim or fad.

I once did a house for a couple who lived in New Jersey and had a son at Dartmouth. Their trips to New Hampshire were spent making lists of literally hundreds of minute details they wished to see incorporated into their new house. Instead of being overwhelmed by their specifications for the height and length of every single towel bar, the layout of every closet, complete with hanging bar and shelf arrangement, and the location of every electrical outlet throughout the entire house, I was delighted. This couple ended up with a house in which practically every detail was exactly as they wanted it because they had thought it out ahead of time.

Another client sent me a voluminous list of items on scratch paper with the following memo:

> Clara and I have scribbled down some notes about our house which may simply confuse you but, if recognized as simply a stream of often inconsistent thoughts, they may be of some help, and even guidance. As you will note, some of the notes refer to houses discussed in clippings that we have saved over the years.

This is, of course, a very effective way for me to learn what my clients are like, whether I have known them before or not. The marginal notations and afterthoughts are often extremely helpful, and in some ways it is better if the notes are handwritten rather than typed because they are apt to be more spontaneous.

Whether you describe your requirements verbally or graphically, by "bubble diagrams" (rough sketches showing the relationship between different rooms) or by lengthy written descriptions, as much data as possible should be provided for the architect's mental computer to sort out.

This information should be spontaneous and uninhibited. Some clients subconsciously attempt to say what they think will please or impress the architect, but an honest expression of ideas is important at this stage, no matter how eccentric or impossible some may seem. You should not assume the architect will scorn your wilder notions, as a good architect does not reject any idea categorically without respectful consideration. What's wrong with a car wash in the garage, a horse stall next to the kitchen counter with an opening for the horse's head, a firemen's pole, lookout towers, drawbridges—why not? Even I have some secret panels and a secret passage in my own house!

As an architect, I am often asked "What kind of house would you design if you could do anything you wanted to?" The response is that I would rather have a *real* problem to solve for clients who know what they want, even if it is relatively modest in scope. It is the limitations rather than the freedoms which are challenging to an architect and stimulating to his inventive talents. Architecture is not an abstract art; it is a social art. The design of a particular house succeeds only insofar as it enriches the life of a family by its response to that family's collective idiosyncrasies. The solution must transcend mere physical comforts and shelter and respond empathetically to the owners' subjective needs as well.

The House Called Cedarfield

A couple I shall call the Burtons (to preserve their privacy) asked me to design a house for them—basically a "core" house which could be expanded—in a rural area about 50 miles from New York City. Though they had no preconceived idea as to what the house should look like, they were very articulate about their needs and what they wanted from the house. They knew how they wanted it to function.

It was an interesting commission for many reasons, and I will use their house to illustrate the process of building at each successive stage. So, first, a little bit about them.

Tricia Burton and I had known each other from childhood. We shared an interest in ballads and folk songs, and we both enjoyed working with wood. She became an accomplished etcher and has written extensively about the history of printmaking.

Her husband, Dave, is a consulting economist who resigned from his firm in New York City just as the construction phase of the house started and relocated his practice to "Cedarfield" the minute it was finished. He is a specialist in his field, so it was feasible for him to practice from his study, although not without some atypical distractions for a distinguished New York City economist. (One client calling him on his New York City tie line and hearing the barking of a dog asked incredulously, "What on earth is that?" "Cinnamon's treed a cat in the mulberry tree," replied Dave.) Dave is also a cabinetmaker, a blacksmith, a photographer, an organic gardener, and an accomplished amateur puppeteer.

Even at the age of five, when the house was being planned, their daughter Karen showed every indication of having the same interest as her parents in arts, crafts, and projects of all sorts.

The whole family, therefore, needed room for the flexible arrangement of desks, tables, and benches, with appropriate storage space and proper light. The result of numerous sessions to define and describe in considerable detail the purpose of each space is outlined in the following summary of the functional program for Cedarfield, compiled from notes given to me by the Burtons.

General Character

An unpretentious, comfortably informal house, wedded graciously to the site. One story, but perhaps with a loft or "tree house." Large basement with 8-foot ceilings with good light. Low maintenance inside and out . . . minimum painting and upkeep. Feeling of space important. Well related to the out-of-doors, but a sense of sheltered enclosure is important. A natural wood house with a variety of spaces inside and out. Out of sight of neighboring houses, but perhaps with a hint of its presence from the road.

Entrances

An inviting front door convenient to the guest parking. A comfortable entrance hall with coat closet and powder room (perhaps guest bath?) convenient to the kitchen, but well separated from the living room. Kitchen door near driveway for groceries and garbage. Various garden doors as appropriate. A "mud-room" entrance through the basement. Perhaps a ramp for the tractor, Rototiller, Sunfish, and gardening equipment (even a car on rare occasions)—no outbuildings, if it proves possible to fit everything under house. Access to living level from basement, probably best near the entrance hall.

Kitchen

Large kitchen with eating area. Sunshine important, hence east and south exposure. Access to deck or terrace on south side. Laundry, freezer, wine storage can be in basement if convenient to stairway. No garage; perhaps a trellised carport later on. Low priority if basement "barn" works.

Living/Dining Room

Living room spacious and wonderful to really live in—the "great hall" of manorial days, but comfortably secure when alone with a good book. Separate dining room not necessary if living room is large enough. Perhaps have option to add on some day. No large sit-down dinners planned—buffet if more than six—so kitchen/dining area should be attractive and slightly separate from work area.

Study

A library to be used as Dave's office with a large, built-in desk, a sofa, and an easy chair. Can be small but not confining. Would like a fireplace if possible. Privacy and quiet important—a retreat.

Bedrooms

Master bedroom with separate dressing area. Would like morning sun, but not on driveway side. Sitting area with desk.

Karen's room not large, but with built-in desk and recessed bed alcove. Cozy.

Guest room must double as a workroom or studio. Keep flexible. A sitting room for guests to retreat to. May become Karen's room in future. Perhaps north light and higher ceiling.

Baths

No fancy baths; functional, convenient, and good storage space for towels, linens, medicines.

"Everything Room"

Space to accommodate desks, benches, reference books, sewing tables. Light and airy. Convenient access, but apt to be cluttered from various and sundry projects, so must be able to be closed off. Perhaps should have alcove for extra guests—perhaps children in sleeping bags.

Good storage. Need not have access to outside. Could go on an upper floor if this helps balance the living spaces with the square footage of the basement.

Printmaking Shop

Small, 8 by 10, with natural light. Counter space, shelving, and pegboard. Could be in basement if not too claustrophobic.

Workshop

Workbench, wood storage, flue for future forge; should be in cellar, but not a passageway from outdoor entrance.

Theater

Part of cellar must be 8 feet high, with a 10-foot-by-14-foot platform area for puppeteer's stage. Ample floor space in front for a dozen spectators.

Storage

Storage, storage, storage, and more storage. All as convenient as possible.

Grounds

Cutting garden, vegetable garden, orchard, mulch pile, cold frame, dog run, possible paddock. Future guest house and indoor/outdoor pool (partially therapeutic). Variety of views.

Programmed Spaces

The best way to approach your own functional program is to consider it, as the Burtons did, in terms of zones, or the major areas important to almost every house. These are:

The Main Approach

I have always preferred having only a glimpse of a house from the road. Just a hint of the roof planes and the chimneys is often sufficient. Then, as one turns in at the entrance, the house may be blocked briefly from view, to be seen again toward the end of the drive, with the front door conspicuously and conveniently located by an ample parking area. A sequence of visual experiences such as this, with its disciplined vistas, gives a hint of an intriguing and varied house to follow.

Not every site permits this sequence, however, nor is it by any means an absolute criterion. Though Cedarfield does have an attractive visual sequence in its approach, the Nathans' site warranted two driveways: a back drive leading to the kitchen door, and a relatively short front drive ending at a garden gate. This gate, in effect, is the front door, while the garden can be viewed as part of the house. The entrance to the house itself is secondary and is simply a sliding door to the foyer. (See pages 32 to 35.)

More and more people are quietly turning their backs on the street and are seeking privacy and seclusion in a more insulated domain, no matter how modest the site and budget may be. Perhaps this is because it is reassuring for individuals to be able to control, in a modest way, their own personal world when so much of what is happening outside is completely overwhelming. The broad, sweeping lawns and studied façade of a period house are no longer most people's goal, even if they can afford the initial building price and the continuing maintenance costs.

In general, no matter how secluded a house, a warm and inviting entrance can still be found at the end of the drive and the visitor made to feel welcome. This can be accomplished in any number of ways. In my own house, for example, the front door is recessed, and one literally becomes sheltered by the body of the house even before lifting the knocker. (See page 48.)

Entrances

The front door should open into a hallway or vestibule, with easy and inviting access to the three major zones of the house—the living rooms, the kitchen, and the private spaces. A large coat closet and, ideally, a powder room or guest bath should be located conveniently near the front door.

There are three basic ways of handling the entrance hall, each perfectly valid. One way is to direct attention to a vista through the house toward a garden or view beyond. Alternatively, the view might be totally blocked by the back of a chimney, a wall, or even closet doors, from which the visitor is invited with varying degrees of emphasis to other areas of the house. A dramatic view or space can have a much greater impact if it is "discovered" around a corner or up some stairs.

A third way of arranging the entry is to offer an immediate and welcoming access to the principal living room of the house. This can be accomplished by changes in texture, light, and ceiling height or, in the case of "upside-down" houses such as the Coker house (page 172) and the Bushfield house (pages 86–87), where the living room is on the second floor, the stairs are encountered head on, and the visitor is enticed into ascending with the promise of an intriguing experience.

Any house that does not offer a definite and decisive direction from the entrance hall usually lacks the clarity and crispness of a well-ordered and workable floor plan.

In addition to the front hall, most families prefer to have an additional entrance through a mud room where one can enter with boots, raincoats, snowsuits, skis, sailbags, or dogs, and become "decontaminated" before entering the house proper. It is also a good spot for the washing machine and dryer. It should be convenient to the kitchen and main entry, so that one can get to the private areas without passing through any of the principal rooms.

Kitchen

The kitchen is often called the most important room in the house. Kitchens are not laboratories in which food is prepared; they are more often than not family social centers. Some even have an easy chair or sofa beside the breakfast area, others a greenhouse or sewing alcove. On the other hand, an efficient galley kitchen may be more suitable to some owners. Some kitchens are open to the living room; these are most successful when the appliances and countertops are blocked from view. Think carefully about all the various possibilities before deciding what suits you best.

Most clients who feel strongly about the way a kitchen should be arranged have probably become accustomed to one particular layout and tend to reproduce the familiar relationship between refrigerator, sink, and range in a new house, even though such an arrangement may be inefficient. If your architect comes up with a new arrangement, try to be open-minded. You may end up with your prescribed design, but be sure it is the result of objective analytical study rather than of habit.

The main approach to the Kellogg house along a winding country road. Built directly behind an existing garage, the house is "discovered" by the visitor.

Above: *The house is first glimpsed from the road and then lost from view.*

Right: *The driveway ends by the garage, and the visitor is invited up the short path to the front door.*

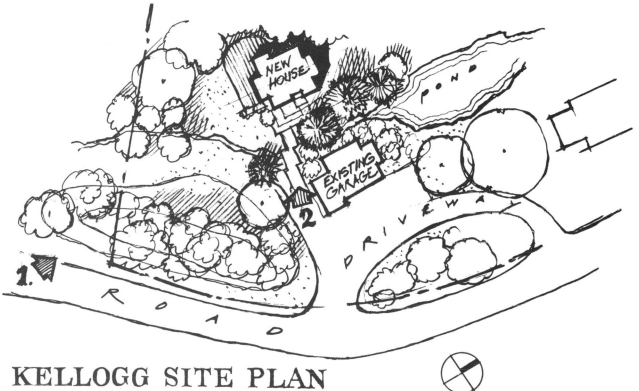

KELLOGG SITE PLAN

NATHANS

An enticing view of the water was gained by placing the main living and the master bedroom on the second and third floors.

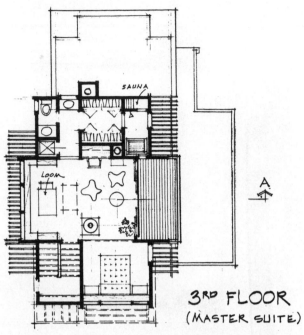

3RD FLOOR
(MASTER SUITE)

SECTION A-A

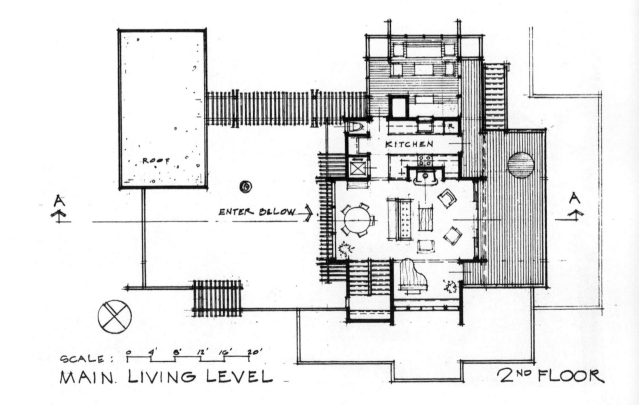

A

ENTER BELOW →

SCALE: 0 4' 8' 12' 16' 20'

MAIN. LIVING LEVEL

2ND FLOOR

Above: *The Nathans house as viewed from the entrance garden. Note the entrance hall beyond the sliding glass doors. (See also pages 38 and 46.)*

Below: *View of the Nathans house as seen from the driveway.*

ENTRANCES

Above: *The entrance to Cedarfield is brightened by light from a clerestory window overhead. One's eye is arrested by the handsome chest against the brick chimney and is then drawn to the living room beyond.*

Left: *The bridge to the Baekeland house is part of the approach sequence seen on pages 162–67.*

Opposite page: *The entrance hall of the Paschal house, looking toward the front door. A gracious formality is still one of the options in a contemporary house.*

KITCHENS
Above: *The Nathans kitchen is visually part of the living space—*
even the shelves are open to view (see also pages 34, 35, and 46).

Above: *The kitchen in the Silvers' beach house is almost a part of the living space (see pages 180–83).*

Below: *The Herzog kitchen carries out the same design details as the rest of the house (see pages 44 and 168–71).*

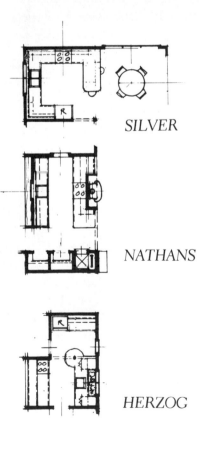

SILVER

NATHANS

HERZOG

One more suggestion: have plenty of light—both daylight and artificial—but think twice about that window over the sink. You can always have it if you insist, but a cupboard over the sink is an excellent place for glasses and storage. You probably will have a dishwasher and spend more time preparing meals than washing up, anyhow, so why not put the window over the counter where you work?

Dining Areas

Most clients include a separate dining room in their original list of requirements, but it is often the first thing to go if there is a budget squeeze. Formal dining rooms often go unused for weeks on end, and the investment in expensive space is more or less wasted.

In our house people are always dropping by, so we use our dining room for meals at least once every day during the week and for three meals a day on weekends. It is not just a dining room, however, except when a meal is actually in progress. It is a passage to the deck, which makes it handy for buffet meals; it is also open to the living room, which lends a feeling of space to both rooms. Its actual square footage is quite small, but it is sunny and open during the day and yet has an elusive quality of intimacy at night, when it is within sound of the living-room fireplace. Its acoustics somehow make it conducive to conversation and, as we love to talk in our house, we find ourselves sitting there literally for hours. (See page 43.)

It is important to have a space that responds to the different demands of the family at different times of the day and seasons of the year. The intimacy of the cozy restaurant does not always work at home. The best dining spaces, whether separate or connected with another room, are generally expansive; sometimes they are high, sometimes low, but they should always be centripetal in their principal focus, with enough flexibility and versatility to create the right atmosphere for a stimulating social occasion.

Group-Living Rooms

Group-living rooms include the standard living room, family room, playroom, and library. The formality or informality of any one of these rooms is a matter of personal preference and life-style, but these rooms should be adaptable spaces that can change with the seasons as well as with your moods, whims, and shifts in life-style. In planning your own group-living areas, a detailed list or description of your family's activities will not only be a great help to your architect, but will also give you a chance to review what is most important to each member of the family.

Insist on flexible, well-thought-out furniture arrangements, all shown in scale, even at the earliest sketch stage of design. Successful furnishing is fundamental to the merit of any room and should dictate the design of the room—not the other way around.

Private Rooms

Adjacent bedrooms and private studies should be separated by closet walls or bathrooms to muffle sounds and ensure privacy. Whatever their size, they should be flexible so they can be adapted as children grow up or circumstances change.

Bedrooms, particularly children's rooms, should be designed for fun. Children need a sense of their own worth and deserve a room uniquely theirs. Children's rooms need not be large, but they should be attractive places for five-year-olds to play in, and adaptable to a sociable teenager's needs.

Guest rooms as such often lie fallow and can easily double as a study or sewing room. Work counters can be recessed into wide closets with shelves or pegboard above. Then they can easily be closed to hide the mess whenever necessary.

Retreats, towers, and assorted window seats, inglenooks, and little lofts and balconies are all great places to retreat to with a good book, or maybe just for a snooze. They add a variety of vistas, scale, and spaces to answer the moods of the owners without adding substantially to the cost of the house. Challenge your architect!

Special Rooms and Outbuildings

Studios, workrooms, wine cellars, exercise rooms, and shops are all possibilities to consider in a building program, and they should be carefully analyzed relative to other spaces. No matter how far away from the house they are, sheds, stables, playhouse, tennis court, even the gazebo, are important factors in the overall design and should be considered integral parts of the whole.

DINING AREAS

Above and left: *Two views of the Coker dining room. The openness of the upper view with its large expanse of glass is balanced by the solidity and warmth of the fireplace mass. The kitchen can just be seen in the lower view (see also page 175).*

Opposite page: *View of the author's dining room with the living room beyond (see page 198).*

GROUP LIVING

Above: *The Tuckerman living room as seen from the entrance hall (see pages 192–95).*

Opposite page: *The Herzog living room as seen from the dining area (see pages 39 and 168–71).*

Right: *The informality of the Regan family room is shown in contrast to the Tuckerman living room (see page 146).*

PRIVATE ROOMS

Above: *The Nathans wanted their own retreat on the third floor of their house: a sleeping alcove, a sitting area with a small balcony, a place for Dr. Nathans's study and Mrs. Nathans's loom (see pages 34, 35, and 38).*

Left: *The Paschals' daughter wanted her bed raised up high with space below for her desk and shelves for her riding trophies.*

Storage

Contemporary houses rarely have attics, mainly because the open space under the roof can usually be put to much better use for living than for storage. A well-planned house should literally have the proverbial "place for everything and everything in its place." Every possession, from the teaspoons to the snowplow, should have a proper storage space, and in planning your house you should catalog virtually everything you own to determine the most suitable location for it.

In addition to coat closets, utility closets, and kitchen/dining storage areas, the living areas of a house often have a liquor closet and bar, and a place for games, card tables, projectors, screens, and junk of all sorts. If there is a fireplace, a woodbox is essential, preferably one that can be loaded from the outside or from a shed, and unloaded next to the fireplace.

Children's rooms need storage places for their toys and belongings. Every bathroom should have a cupboard for supplies, and no matter how large the linen closet may be, it will always get filled with something. Each person's clothes closet should be designed to accommodate his or her particular needs. When you have allocated all the space you'll need for the bicycles, the minitractor, and such items as outgrown clothes and the broken antique chair you intend to repair some day, add another good-sized storage room that is at least 30 square feet (50 is better) for general storage, excluding the specialized closets already mentioned.

General Character

Sometimes a descriptive phrase or a single suggestive word can encapsulate the intended spirit of the house—"a rustic retreat," "a romantic incident in nature," "a contemporary saltbox." Perhaps some people still subscribe to Le Corbusier's notion that a house is a "machine for living."

The more analytical you, as a client, can be, the more you know what you want because of a commitment to a life-style that is uniquely yours, then the more stimulating the challenge to the architect's creative and interpretive ability. Just because you hire an architect to "do" a house doesn't mean he should do all the work!

There is a tendency on the part of clients who have done a lot of homework—who have pictures of houses that are "exactly" right and

View of the front entrance of the author's house.

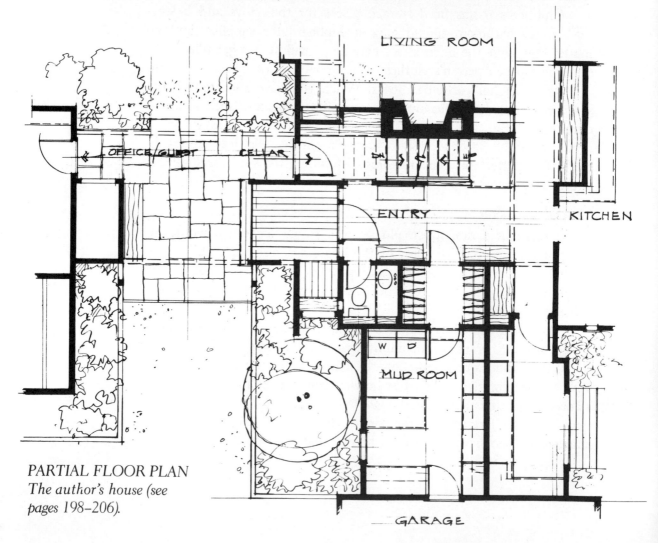

LIVING ROOM

OFFICE/GUEST   CELLAR

ENTRY   KITCHEN

MUD ROOM

GARAGE

PARTIAL FLOOR PLAN
The author's house (see
pages 198–206).

even layouts they have developed for themselves—to fall in love with "their" solutions. These sketches should be no more than a starting point for a design, and they may not always work out. Try to be dispassionate about "your" design. It is the architect's job to synthesize your ideas and develop a solution based on your program, but tempered by his own sense of design, structure, and order within the parameters of your taste and character.

A house that is too contrived, too preciously self-conscious in its geometric discipline, can be interesting as sculpture, but stultifying to live in, as the needs of its human inhabitants are subordinated to structure. It may be difficult to alter or add to it at a future time without sacrificing the integrity of its form. On one occasion when I was a guest at such a house, designed by an architect for himself, one of his other guests asked whether it would destroy the composition if she moved her chair. Her remark made that contemporary living room suddenly seem as rigid and stultifying as a Victorian parlor on Sunday!

The character of a house may be compared to that of a person. The social buffoon who is susceptible to every fad that comes along and who uses continuous clichés is extremely tiresome. No matter how provocative his appearance and views, he wears very thin after a while. Quite simply, he becomes a bore—as does the house built as the modish *tour de force* that ends up as a dated cliché, its glitter gone with the passing of time. Houses that wear well are like people who may not seem all that fascinating at first meeting but are the ones who display the most warmth and friendship. Beauty, richness, and charm come from the soul of a person, as does the essence of a house expressed in its form, its texture, and its lack of pretentious veneer.

ARCHITECTURAL PROGRAM

Throughout the development of the functional program for most houses, the tentative size of various rooms is generally considered. But when the functional program is completed, a second phase, the architectural program, begins, during which square footage is more definitely decided upon. At this time the client and architect work together, discarding elements from the earlier program that are no longer necessary or desirable, outlining more specific spaces, and assigning appropriate square footage to these spaces.

The architectural program for Cedarfield is shown as an example in the following table. If you compare it with the functional program, you will see that we managed to include all the desired areas, though the size of the basement dictated a separate story for the project room.

ARCHITECTURAL PROGRAM FOR CEDARFIELD

Spaces	Notes	Approximate Size (in feet)	Gross Square Footage
Above Grade:			
Entrance Hall	w/closet	10 × 14	150
Living-Dining	w/fireplace	20 × 30	625
Kitchen	w/dining	14 × 18	250
Study	w/fireplace	14 × 14	200
Master Bedroom	w/desk space and dressing	14 × 28	300
Bath	w/storage	10 × 10	100
Karen's Bedroom	w/dressing	12 × 14	175
Bath (Karen and Guest)	w/powder room	8 × 10	80
Guest Bedroom (Studio)	w/high ceiling	14 × 14	200
Project Room	2nd floor (?)	14 × 20	280
TOTAL			2,360
Circulation & Unprogrammed Space @ 18% (plus or minus)			440
GROSS SQUARE FOOTAGE ABOVE GRADE			2,800
Basement:			
Open Space—2 car lengths		14 × 40	560
Utility Room—Mud Room		14 × 10	140
Printmaking Shop		10 × 12	120
Theater		16 × 20	320
Workshop		16 × 20	320
Miscellaneous Storage			140
Mechanical Equipment			300
			1,900

In designing your own house, don't worry too much if the total square footage seems small in your architectural program. The more skillfully a house is planned and its spaces molded, the less you need to count square footage as a measure of design. (The living room in my new house is virtually the same square footage as that in my former, renovated house, but my friends won't believe me—it *seems* so much larger because of the way the space is handled. See page 52.)

Though some flexibility is possible even after the design process begins, the more precise the architectural program is in establishing the limits within which the designer must work, the more likely it is that the end product will be a unified whole. It is also far easier to control the costs if you have a well-thought-out architectural program.

Nothing is more disheartening to an architect than to have an extraneous bit of innocent data interjected as an afterthought when he has already developed a design. Sometimes even the substitution of a tub for a shower stall in the second bathroom can throw a balanced design out of equilibrium. This is an extreme example, but I cannot emphasize enough the importance of resolving the program thoroughly before the architect starts designing.

This is also the stage at which to consider the option of eventual expansion, either for your own needs or for resale. So often houses that are "too perfect" are so static in the rigidity of their design that the traumatic impact of adding a wing at some future time destroys the sculptural integrity of the house. With rising costs, a young couple may well want a two-stage house—one which can grow with a growing family as economic conditions allow. The Losquadro house, for example, was built for a young couple with no children who wanted the option of adding a wing later on as their family grew, or as a selling point if they ever moved. (See page 53.)

In determining the cost of a house three factors must be taken into consideration: its size, the quality and cost of its materials, and its budget. The owner can, and should, control any two of these, but the architect must have leeway and discretion with the third. In other words, if you insist on a house of a certain size using specified materials, these two factors will determine the cost to a very large extent. If the budget and the size are both rigid, the cost of the materials must be flexible, and if materials and budget are "given," the size of the house has to be subject to change.

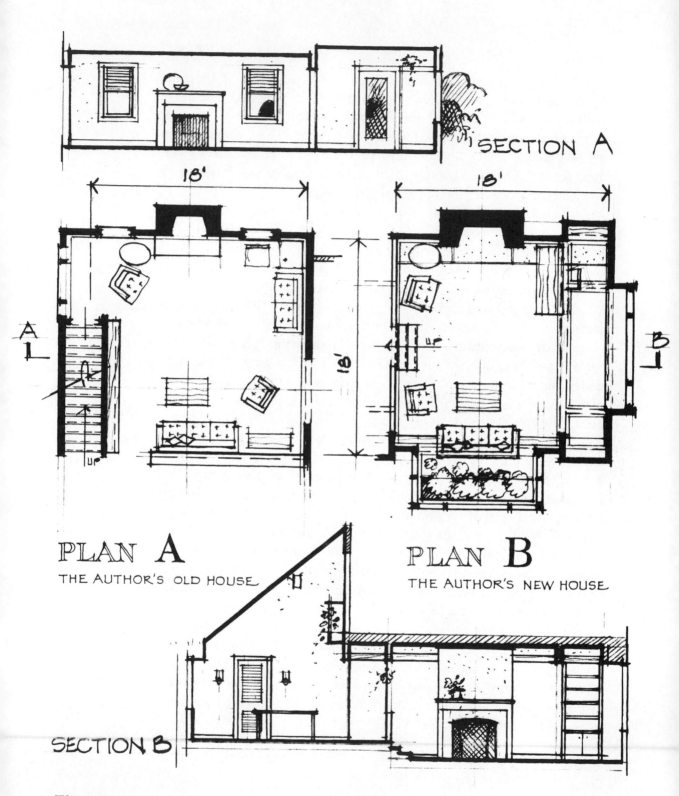

SECTION A

18'

18'

A

B

PLAN A

THE AUTHOR'S OLD HOUSE

PLAN B

THE AUTHOR'S NEW HOUSE

SECTION B

The author's new living room seems much larger than his old one because of the increase in volume and vista.

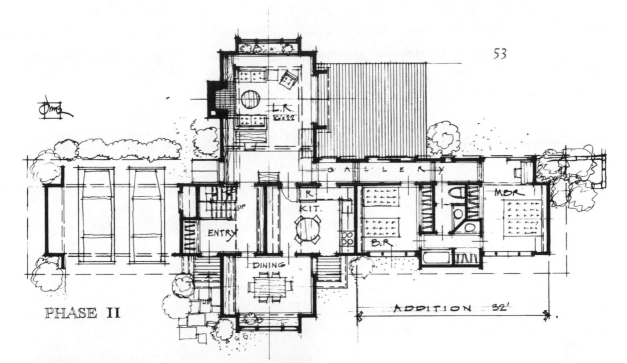

PHASE II

LOSQUADRO HOUSE

This house was to be built in two stages. A young married couple with no children planned to add two bedrooms and a bath as their family grew.

PHASE I

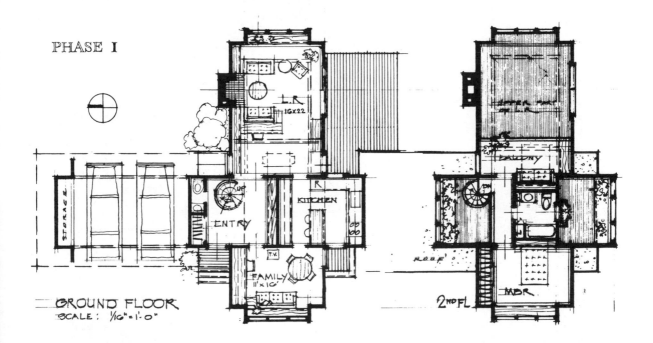

GROUND FLOOR
SCALE: 1/16" = 1'-0"

2ND FL

Above: *Partial view of the Cedarfield site seen from the west ten years before construction. (Note the cedar tree in the lower left.)*

Below: *Site plan of Cedarfield, showing legal setbacks and proposed land use.*

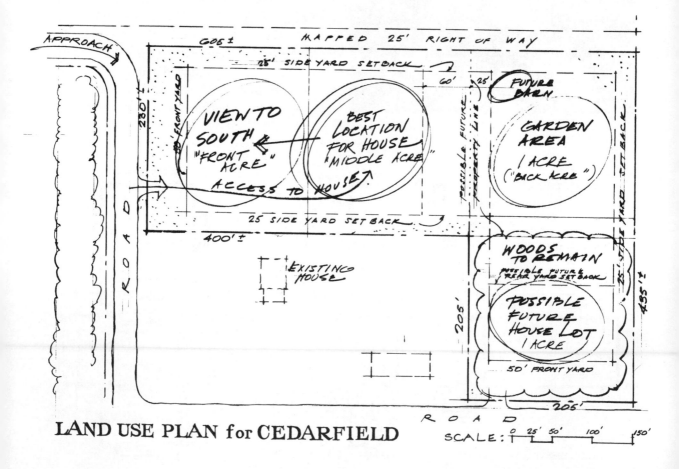

APPROACH

MAPPED 25' RIGHT OF WAY

600'±

25' SIDE YARD SETBACK

280'±

30' FRONT YARD

60'   25'

FUTURE BARN

VIEW TO SOUTH "FRONT ACRE"

BEST LOCATION FOR HOUSE "MIDDLE ACRE"

GARDEN AREA 1 ACRE ("BACK ACRE")

POSSIBLE FUTURE PROPERTY LINE

ACCESS TO HOUSE

25 SIDE YARD SETBACK

400'±

R O A D

EXISTING HOUSE

WOODS TO REMAIN
POSSIBLE FUTURE REAR YARD SETBACK

25' SIDE YARD SETBACK

455'±

POSSIBLE FUTURE HOUSE LOT 1 ACRE

205'

50' FRONT YARD

205'

R O A D

LAND USE PLAN for CEDARFIELD

SCALE: 0 25' 50' 100' 150'

An architect cannot be expected to design a 3,000-square-foot house with fieldstone walls and a copper roof for $200,000. If you insist on fieldstone and copper, the architect must be able to decrease the square footage or increase the budget. If you reject both suggestions, the architect has no alternative but to go to concrete block or some less costly material, or to tell you to forget the whole thing.

Before starting the next phase, therefore, you and your architect should review the ground rules and budget thoroughly. It is often helpful to total the square footage based on room-size requirements (no design necessary), add 20 percent for circulation, and multiply by the local square-foot costs. Though far from perfect, this can at least establish an approximate budget based on your needs.

In the 1920s Frank Lloyd Wright was once asked if he could design a $10,000 house. He replied that he could design a $10,000 house for $10,000, but he could not design a $20,000 house for $10,000. An architect is not a magician, whatever his other qualifications, so have a frank discussion about money before going any further. In spite of horrendous tales you may have heard about overages and the impracticality of architects when it comes to money, do remember it is impossible to design within a budget unless the architect knows what you really intend to spend.

I did a weekend house for a couple several years ago. The husband described a $200,000 house and said they didn't want to spend more than $175,000. I took him at his word. He eventually got his $200,000 house, however, but paid close to $225,000 for it because he "cautiously" added to the house by authorized changes. The change orders constantly broke the contractor's momentum and resulted in costly delays and frustrating crises.

Once a program has been decided upon, complete with alternatives and options, it is your responsibility to supply the architect with a topographical survey of the site, showing trees and rocks, together with a description of any legal encumbrances that may exist. Though the architect may well have the zoning and building codes for the area (available from the local building department, usually located in the town hall), you should supply this as well if the site is outside the architect's general area.

Now that the "problem" of your house has been articulated the architect can begin to seek a design solution within the constraints of program, site, codes, and cost.

A Hell's Angel needs a large garage, a small kitchen and a library of one book (Ma Bell's), yet an appropriate vehicle—architecturally speaking—could be designed.

John P. T. Blake

2 THE SOLUTION
The Design—The Architect's Domain

Once the program has been defined the architect really goes to work. Though he will consult with the owner and sometimes the builder, this phase is properly dominated by the architect. Without romanticizing the architectural process, "inspiration" does play a role in the initial stage. The architect's imagination and his creative and interpretive talents combine with his engineering skills to produce a solution to the owner's problem that exploits the natural felicitous features of the site, while deemphasizing its drawbacks. He molds the design to express the problem, primarily tempered by his personal taste and artistic predilections, yet disciplined by the constraints of the assigned budget.

Any utilitarian structure that physically functions as a shelter is a building, but it is not necessarily architecture. Architecture as a fine art transcends building. Although a precise definition of contemporary architecture is elusive, I would regard a contemporary house as successful if it were functional in its physical conformation and satisfying in its response to a sense of cultural and environmental order. This can be accomplished by the manner in which the building expresses its nature and the materials from which it is made. In a successful building, space becomes as much a reality as the elements which define it. The seeds of an architectural solution should lie within the nature of the problem itself, and the result should not be imposed to comply with some stylistic dogma or influenced by a predetermined set of formulae. A tract builder's replica of Mount Vernon and a manneristic copy of a

Phillip Johnson glass house are buildings but not architecture because neither house is a response derived from its own program or problem.

The architectural design process is threefold. The American Institute of Architects (A.I.A.) defines these phases as "Schematic Design," "Design Development," and "Construction Documents," to which might be added instruction sheets and supplementary drawings made during construction. The first phase covers the conception of a design, the second its development and growth, and the third its refinement and the clarification of details, but all these phases are part of the same process, which constitutes the bulk of the architect's creative work. I will discuss each phase in sequence to illustrate and clarify what happens and to indicate what you should expect from the architect as the design progresses.

SCHEMATIC DESIGN PHASE

The schematic design phase is divided into two parts: the basic concept of the house expressed in what is called a "parti," and its initial development graphically in schematic drawings.

Parti

The first goal of an architect in designing a house is to develop the parti (pronounced par-tee). A parti is simply a basic statement of policy or direction expressed graphically. It is a commitment to an idea —the "germ of an idea"—which is the seed of the whole scheme. Although there may not necessarily be any indication of a house's eventual mass or shape in a parti, there is a *resolution* of basic circulation patterns, orientation, and number of stories. (The term *parti* comes from the French word for "resolution," originally given its architectural meaning at the Ecole de Beaux Arts in Paris.)

The parti, then, is the architect's innovative and coordinative interpretation of how spaces within the proposed house should be arranged and is a direct synthesis of the elements of both the functional and the architectural programs that takes into account the features of the particular site.

There is an elusive aesthetic potential inherent in the parti, but it is chiefly determined by the following objective considerations:

> Program
> Approach and relation to road
> Terrain with special features
> Orientation
> View
> Climate
> Utilities
> Neighborhood
> Codes and zoning regulations

In contemporary residential work there should be virtually no consideration at this stage of a predetermined shape, form, or style.

I can't overemphasize the importance of the parti. The architect should review the logic of each step in its conception thoroughly with you so that its basic assumptions and principles are consistent, at least in theory, with your views. A two-story solution might be anathema to you, and a parti rejected for that reason alone.

The creation of the parti is a terribly important step in the design process and one you as a client are not apt to appreciate unless you have had prior experience trying to resolve so complex a problem as the interrelationships of the elements of a single family house. This is even more difficult than it might appear at first glance, for an architect is able to envision a much more complicated and challenging set of problems to be solved than a layman can because the architect's background has taught him to respect so many considerations that will never be enumerated in any program, no matter how thoroughly it is conceived.

In this phase the traditional image of the gentle muse is far less accurate than that of an elusive and diabolically mischievous imp, who dances through a maze, offering tantalizing clues to a solution, but concealing the final key until he is captured, tethered, and subdued by the exhausted but determined architect.

An architect whose standards of achievement are high can struggle for days, perhaps weeks, trying to develop a parti for even a fairly simple residence. With a final shriek of "Eureka!" he may rush to share his discovery with you, and all that you may see is a scribbled diagram on a piece of scruffy paper. You may stare at your professional adviser as if he had taken leave of his senses and wonder what on earth all this fuss is over a doodle on a bit of scratch paper.

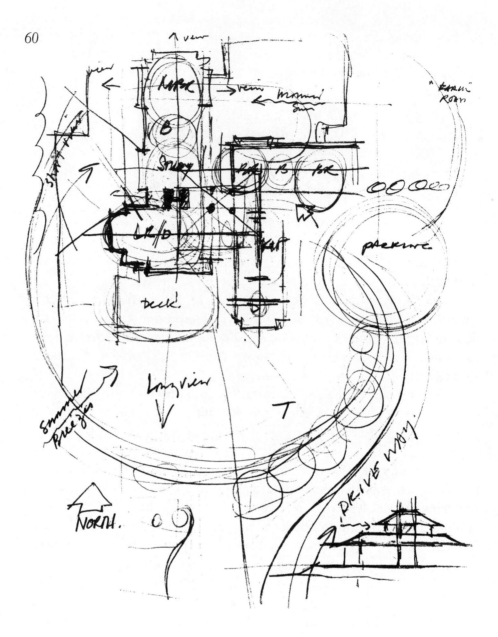

PARTI OF CEDARFIELD. *Original concept of Cedarfield, showing a general grouping of the spaces in relation to the site. There is a vague suggestion of volume in the section at the lower right corner.*

Opposite page: *"Thumbnail" sketches of Cedarfield which explain the concept of the parti and indicate its possible development.*

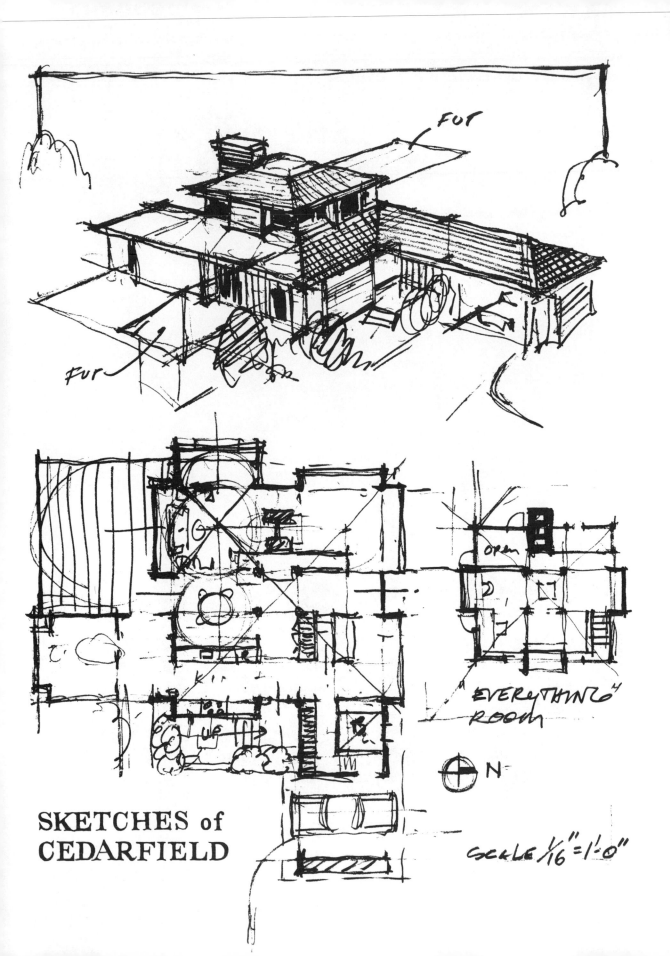

FUT

FUT

OPEN

EVERYTHING
ROOM

KIT

UP

N

**SKETCHES of
CEDARFIELD**

SCALE 1/16" = 1'-0"

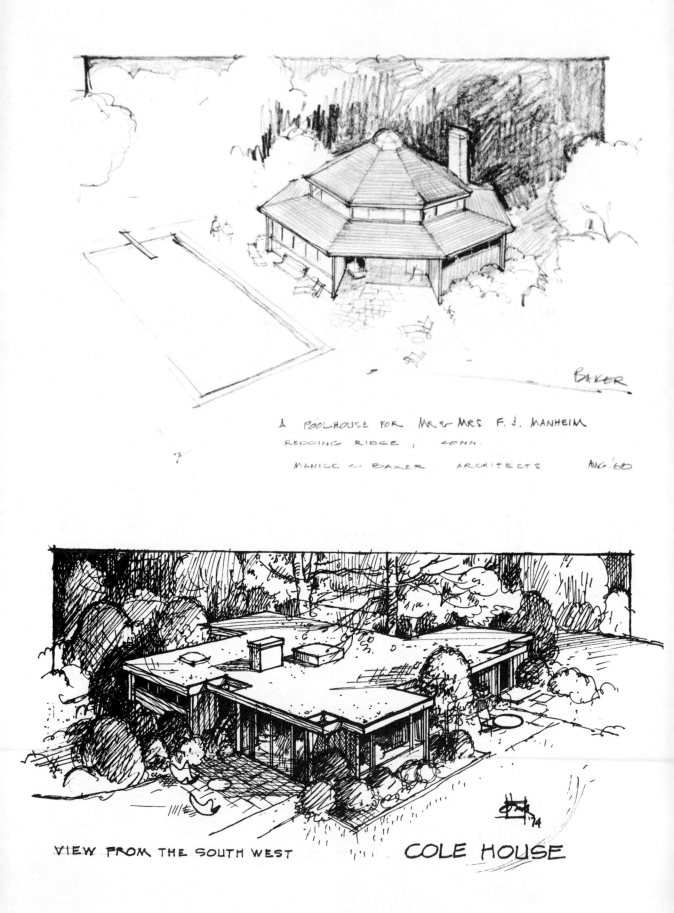

BAKER

A POOLHOUSE FOR MR & MRS F. J. MANHEIM
REDDING RIDGE, CONN.
MANICE & BAKER ARCHITECTS AUG '60

VIEW FROM THE SOUTH WEST   COLE HOUSE

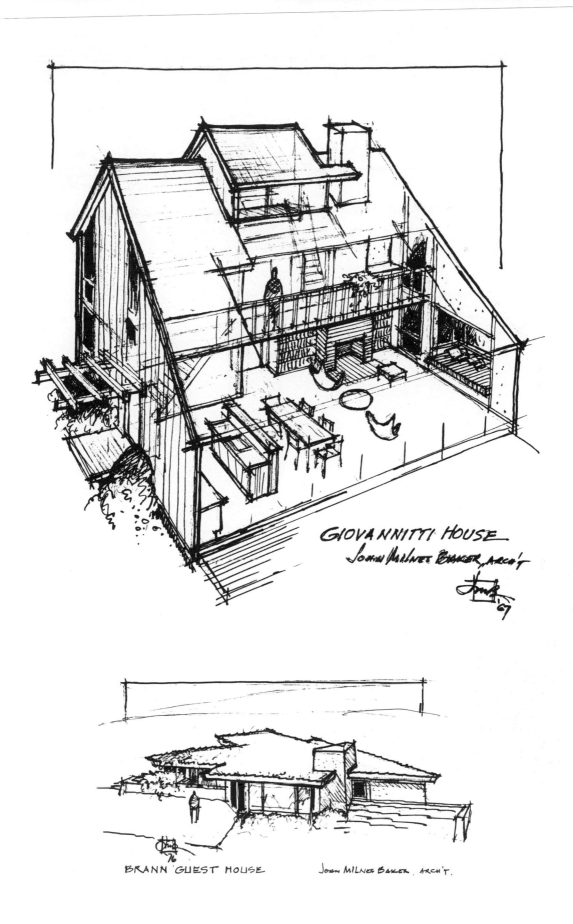

GIOVANNITTI HOUSE

John Milner Baker, Arch't

BRANN GUEST HOUSE   John Milner Baker, Arch't.

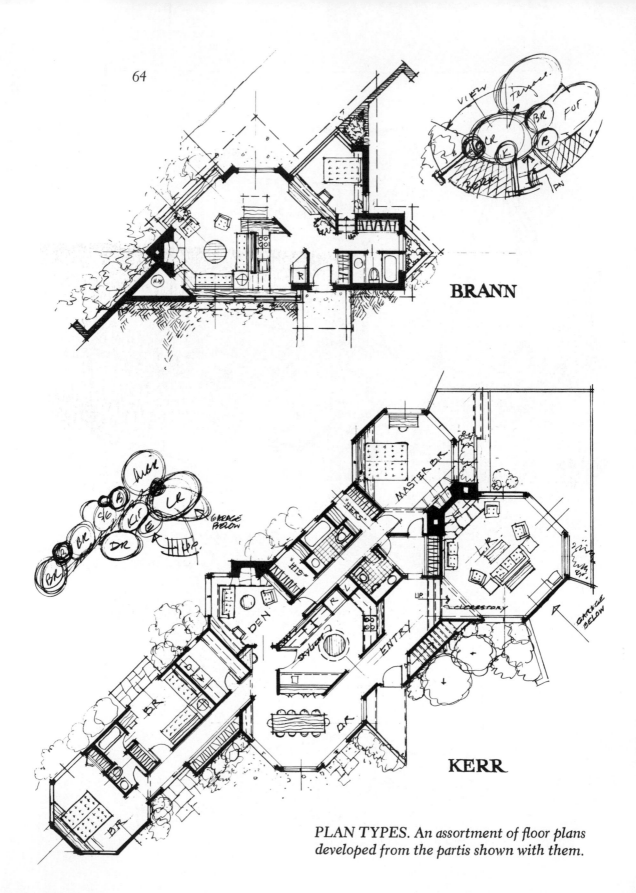

BRANN

KERR

PLAN TYPES. *An assortment of floor plans developed from the partis shown with them.*

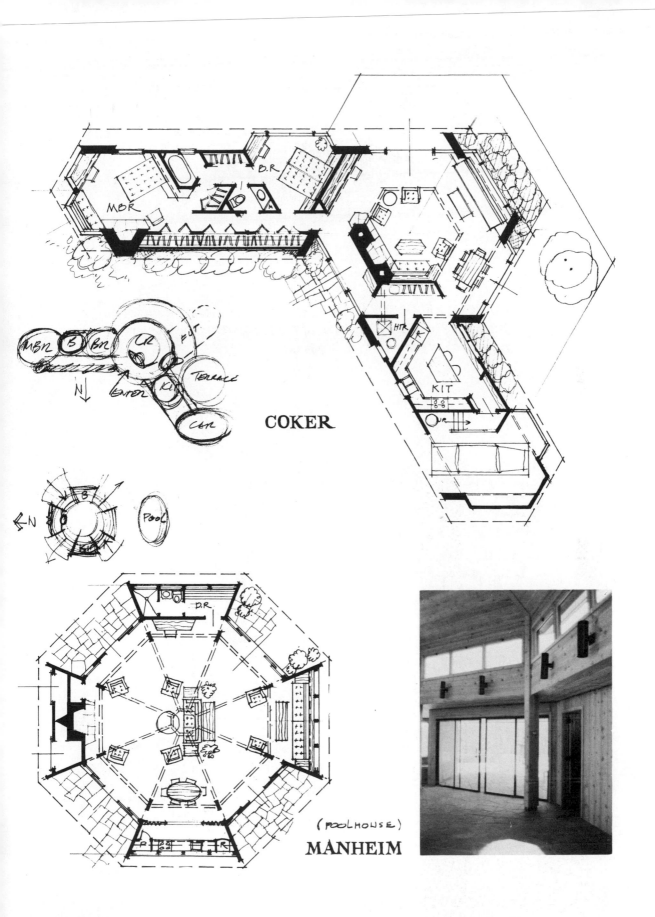

COKER

(POOLHOUSE)
MANHEIM

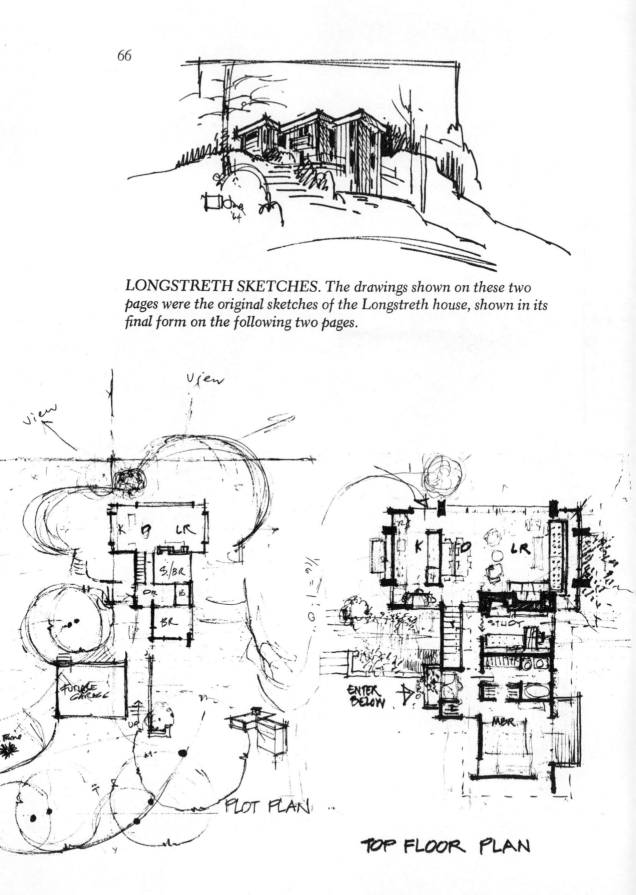

LONGSTRETH SKETCHES. *The drawings shown on these two pages were the original sketches of the Longstreth house, shown in its final form on the following two pages.*

PLOT PLAN

TOP FLOOR PLAN

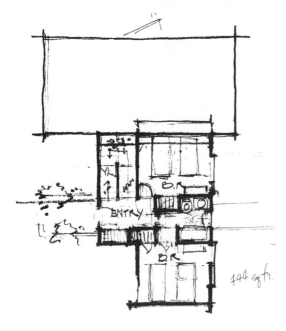

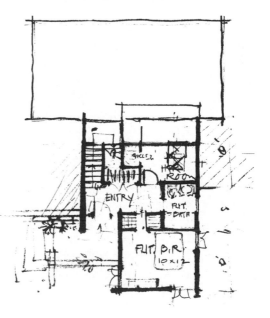

SECOND FLOOR PLAN   LOWER FLOOR PLAN

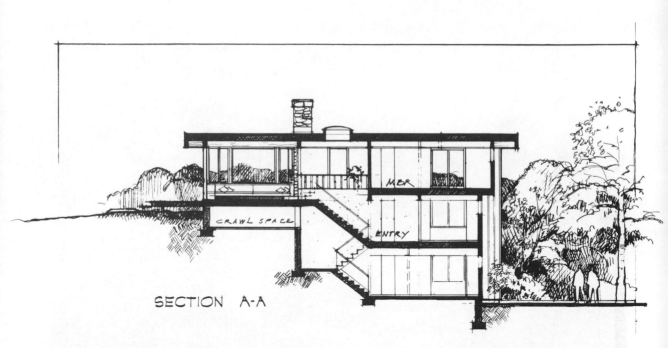

SECTION A-A

LONGSTRETH HOUSE. *Though the basic concept of the house did not change, many subtle modifications during the development of the preliminaries and the working drawings contributed to the more cohesive quality of the final design.*

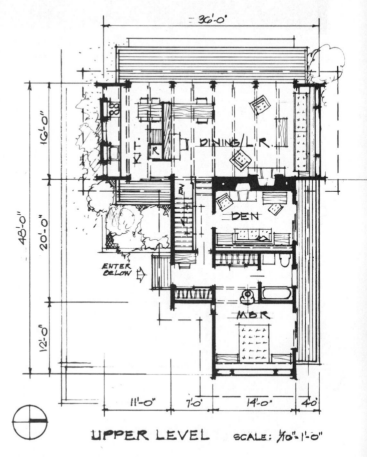

UPPER LEVEL   SCALE: ⅒"=1'-0"

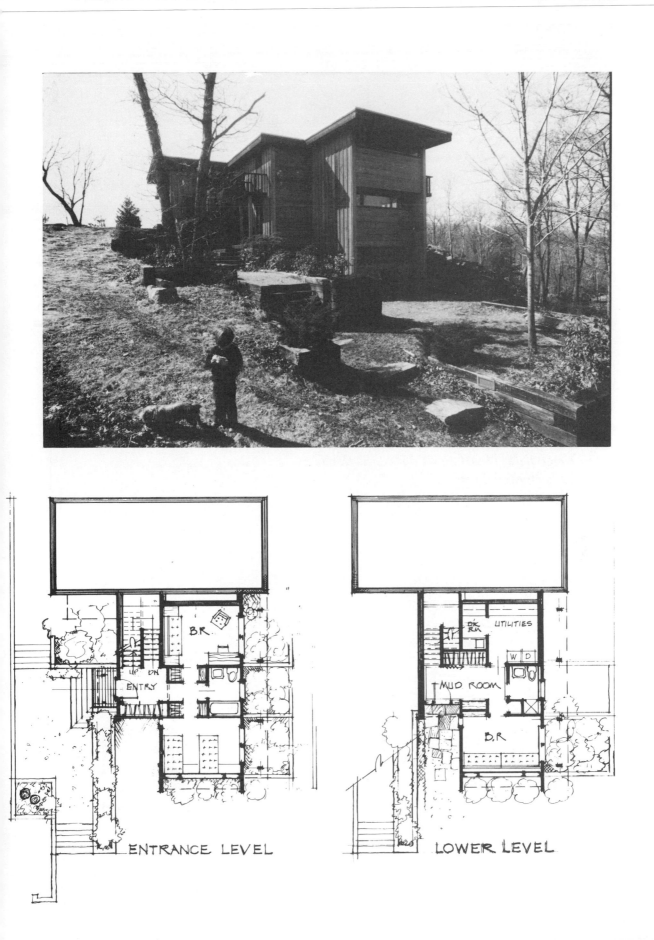

ENTRANCE LEVEL   LOWER LEVEL

2ND FL

1ST FL

WALL HOUSE. *The similarity in spirit between the original sketch stage and the completed house is illustrated here. This design fulfilled the Walls' desire for a "mini Irish castle."*

A HOUSE FOR
MR & MRS JOAN T. WALL

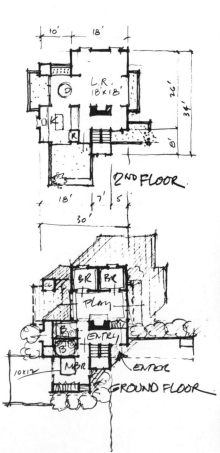

2ND FLOOR

GROUND FLOOR

It is difficult to realize that there may be more content and potential depth in that doodle than anyone outside the profession could ever imagine. This strange, intuitive process, perhaps the single most creative step in the entire design process, is extremely difficult to explain to the person who asks, "How do you know what to draw?" The usual answer is: "I don't know, I just get an idea." Consequently, most architects will not show the parti itself to the client, but rather an amplification of it in the form of sketches.

You may be confused and dismayed if the architect confronts you immediately with a rough sketch, so it is often better for the architect to sketch step by step, on a large pad, the sequential considerations which led to the final solution. As the architect adds element to element and demonstrates the careful logic of a scheme which may have come to him intuitively, perhaps after many sleepless nights, the order and inevitability of the design become apparent. In this way you can participate vicariously in the creative process to a considerable degree, and your resulting sense of involvement will be satisfying to you and stimulating to the architect.

Schematics

If the solution to a complex problem exists in the parti created by the architect as artist, it is the architect as craftsman who nurtures and controls its development.

Once the sketches have been reviewed by you, the client, and modifications and adjustments suggested and approved, then the design takes on an energy and direction of its own and literally almost designs itself. The architect becomes a mere draftsman drawing lines dictated by a force within the idea, which now reveals the image of form, much as the wire armature on which a clay sculpture will be modeled offers a hint of its final shape.

The drawings which will be formally submitted to you for your approval at the schematic stage are not precise or detailed, but pictorial and impressionistic. Solids and planes are indicated, but the textures and materials do not matter at this point; it would be the same house with shingles or "tongue and groove" wood siding. Voids and openings are shown, but whether the windows are aluminum or wood, or whether they open out or slide is not of urgent consequence. These details are usually examined at the later design-development stage. The schematic phase is still largely conceptual in nature; dimensions, proportions, and sometimes basic structural systems have yet to be defined. Even such a basic decision as to whether a roof is to be flat or pitched is still open for discussion.

At this point you may be overly impressed by the graphic quality of the presentation, but you must make a determined effort not to be seduced by the visual devices and to evaluate the solution carefully. Presentation techniques should be used by architects to explain and clarify a design, not to sell it. If you have any doubts about the design, now is the time to discuss changes, because if you make any basic changes after accepting the schematics, you will be liable for an additional fee to cover the time the architect spends in redesign.

A typical set of schematics includes the following drawings:

Site Plan

The site plan is usually drawn at a scale of $\frac{1}{20}$ of an inch per foot or $\frac{1}{16}$ of an inch per foot. This shows the proposed location of the house with respect to the road and the side and rear lot lines, in accordance with the requirements of the local building ordinance. Vistas should be clearly indicated and so should any necessary site work and the proposed placing of the utilities, either on the site or in the street. The plan should be colored or toned so that it can be easily "read."

Floor Plans

At this stage floor plans are usually drawn at $\frac{1}{8}$ of an inch per foot ("eighth-inch scale"), showing key furniture and all exterior openings. Cut lines should be shown, indicating where sectional views are taken.

Sections

Drawn at $\frac{1}{4}$ of an inch per foot ("quarter-inch scale"), sections are views of one part of the building from a plane cut through the entire structure. Sections show relative ceiling heights and changes of level. Key dimensions in the vertical plane should be shown clearly, in addition to human figures and furniture drawn to the correct scale. The spaces revealed in a sectional view usually tell far more about the design than the elevations, which are often omitted at this stage unless they are particularly informative.

NORTH ELEVATION

EAST ELEVATION

SECTIONS AND ELEVATIONS.

*The proposal for a house designed
for the Shreeveses is shown
to illustrate sections and elevations.*

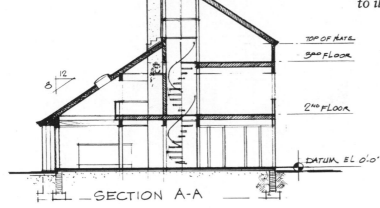

TOP OF PLATE

3RD FLOOR

2ND FLOOR

DATUM EL 0'-0"

SECTION A-A

12
8

3RD FL.

DN

18'-0"

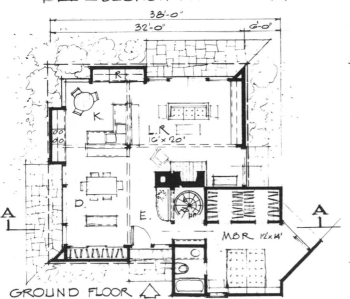

38'-0"

32'-0"   6'-0"

R

K

L.R.
10' x 20'

D

E.

A   A

MBR 12'x14'

GROUND FLOOR

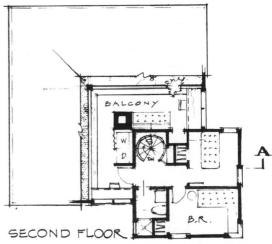

BALCONY

W
D

A

B.R.

SECOND FLOOR

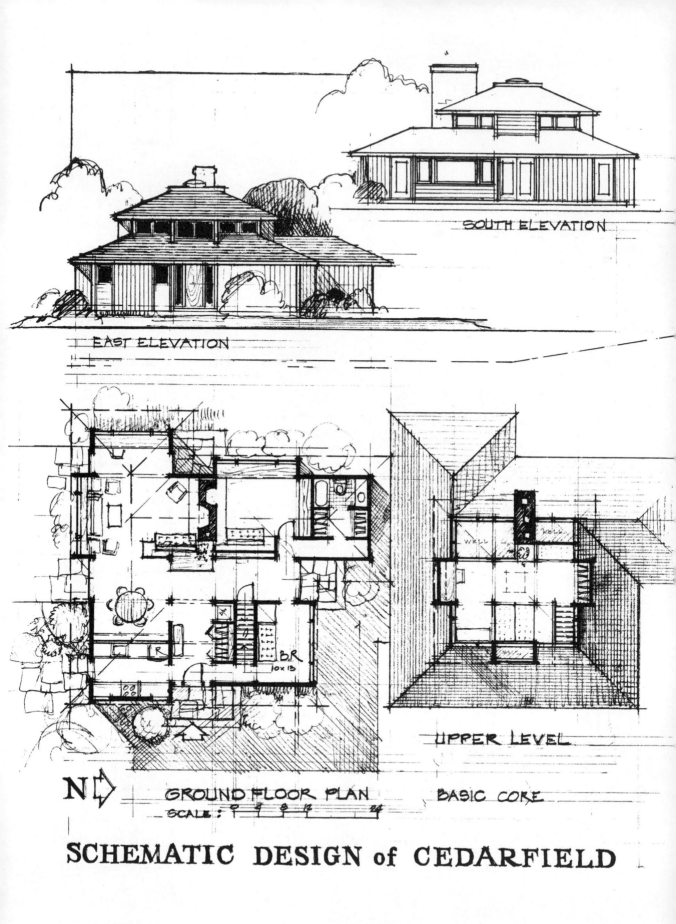

SOUTH ELEVATION

EAST ELEVATION

B.R
10 x 13

WELL

WELL

UPPER LEVEL

N⟩ GROUND FLOOR PLAN BASIC CORE
SCALE:

SCHEMATIC DESIGN of CEDARFIELD

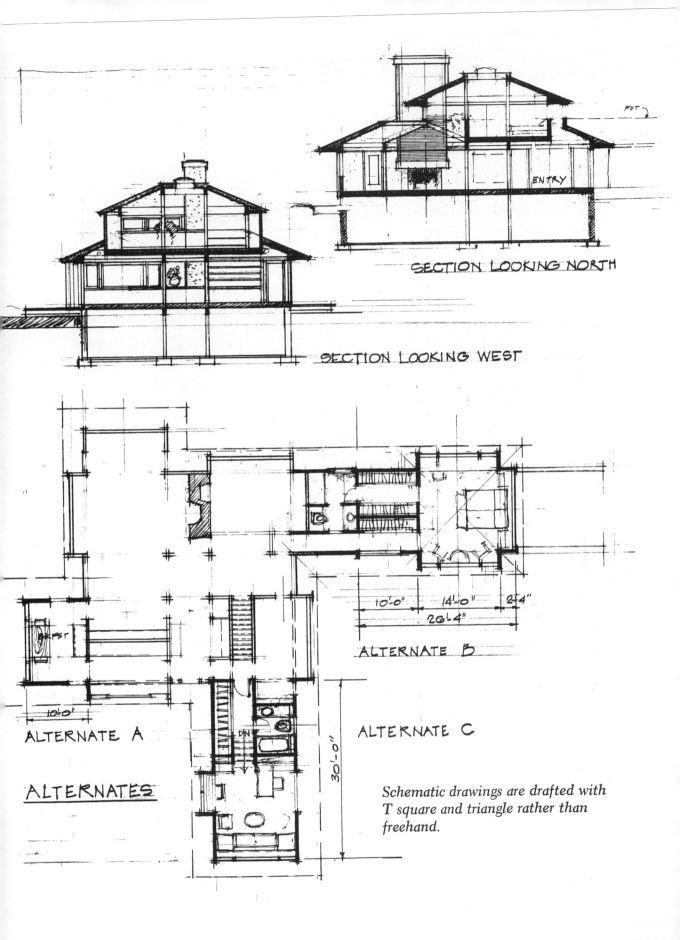

SECTION LOOKING NORTH

ENTRY

SECTION LOOKING WEST

ALTERNATE B

10'-0" 14'-0" 2'-4"
20'-4"

ALTERNATE A

10'-0"

ALTERNATE C

30'-0"

DN

ALTERNATES

Schematic drawings are drafted with T square and triangle rather than freehand.

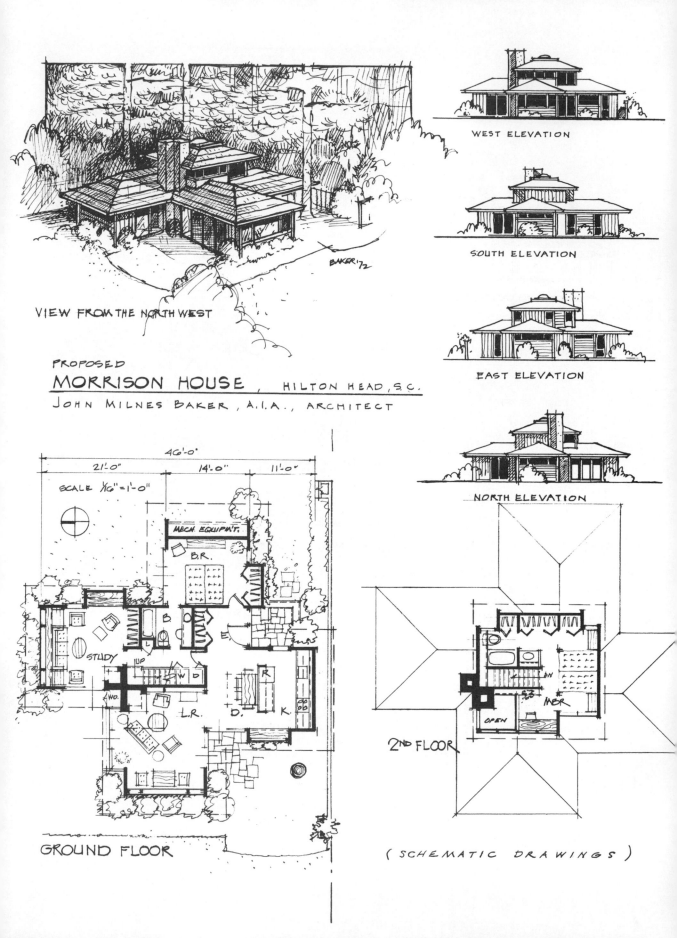

VIEW FROM THE NORTHWEST

PROPOSED
MORRISON HOUSE, HILTON HEAD, S.C.
JOHN MILNES BAKER, A.I.A., ARCHITECT

WEST ELEVATION

SOUTH ELEVATION

EAST ELEVATION

NORTH ELEVATION

46'-0"
21'-0"   14'-0"   11'-0"

SCALE 1/16"=1'-0"

MECH. EQUIP'NT.

B.R.

STUDY

UP

L.R.   D.   K.

GROUND FLOOR

2ND FLOOR

(SCHEMATIC DRAWINGS)

BAKER '72

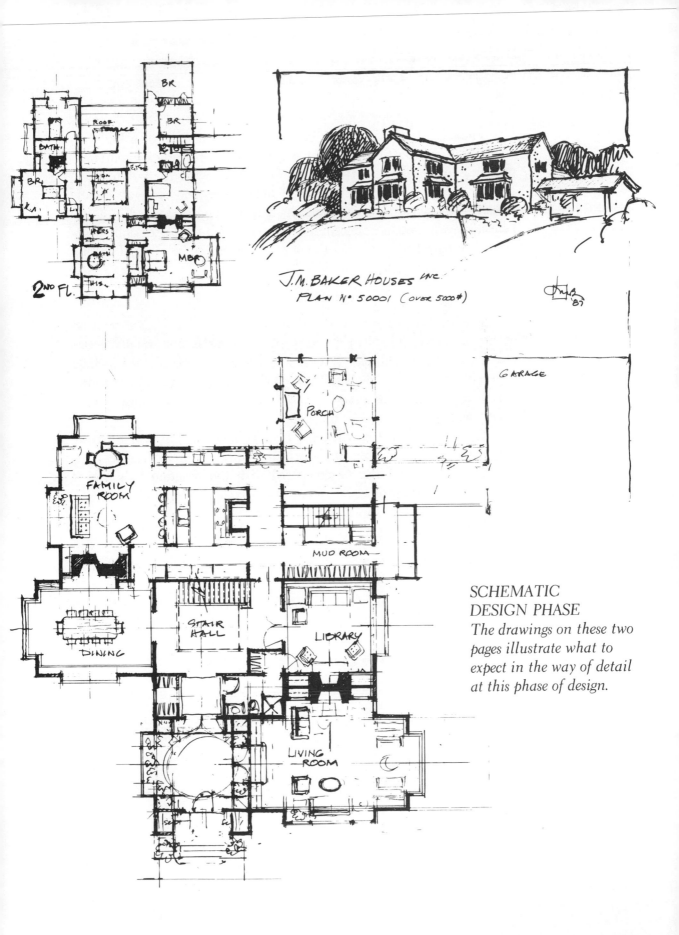

BR

BR

ROOF TERRACE

BATH

BR

BATH

MBR

H.S.

2ND FL.

J.M. BAKER HOUSES INC.
PLAN Nº 50001 (OVER 5000#)

GARAGE

PORCH

FAMILY ROOM

MUD ROOM

DINING

STAIR HALL

LIBRARY

LIVING ROOM

SCHEMATIC
DESIGN PHASE
*The drawings on these two
pages illustrate what to
expect in the way of detail
at this phase of design.*

Elevations

These are two-dimensional orthographic projections of a building. There is no perspective. They are included more to indicate materials, patterns, and proportions than to give an idea of what the building will actually look like. If elevations are included they are, however, usually rendered drawings; that is, they have been colored or shaded and embellished with sketches of scale figures and *entourage* (trees and shrubbery) and have been given a sense of depth by the convention of casting shadows—usually at an angle of 45 degrees.

Perspective Sketches

Sometimes a study model, made of cardboard or clay, is submitted by the architect to explain the massing, but this is not usually necessary. It is, however, absolutely vital that the schematics should include plenty of perspective sketches. These may be rough and impressionistic, but there should be as many of them as are needed to communicate exactly what is envisioned by the architect.

The elements of the schematic design should be checked to see if they fulfill the assumptions implicit in the parti and are within its limitations. They should also be compared with the program to see how effectively the goals which were set at that time have been met.

Evaluating the Schematics

There are certain practical considerations to review at this point. Presumably, by now you have complete faith in your architect as a rational being and a competent professional. Whether this confidence is justified or not depends to a large extent upon how realistically the architect has resolved the problems implicit in the program within the parameters of cost and structural feasibility. This can be determined by a dispassionate and analytical review of the solution shown in the schematics.

On first inspection, the design may appear to be very different from what you envisioned originally, but, upon a closer examination, it should be evident that the outward appearance has been shaped by the elements of the program reflected first in the parti. So if there has been good communication all along between you and your architect, this preliminary design should not be all that surprising.

TELEPHONE NOOK

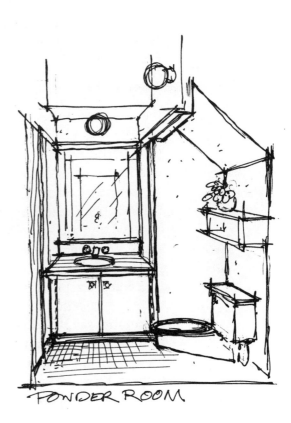

POWDER ROOM

PERSPECTIVE SKETCHES. *The client should be presented with sketches of almost every significant detail in the house. Your architect will draw sketches like these in a matter of minutes—often while you watch.*

JAMIE'S BEDNOOK

By now you should be reassured that the proposed design is a successful interpretation of the physical requirements. If you find the rationale of the design satisfying at this point, there is every reason to believe that the actual appearance of the house can be refined and modified at the development stage to encompass your emotional reaction to the building itself. No architectural design can be appreciated without an understanding of the forces that shaped it, and the more clearly the problems are explained, the greater the appreciation and respect for the solution.

At this point you may well want to take some time to study the solution carefully before proceeding to the next phase. You may even be tempted to show the drawings to friends, but beware of self-styled "experts" in the field of residential design. The design will probably be attacked and praised with little understanding of the problems of program, site, codes, and costs. So do not take your friends' casual and gratuitous advice too seriously; their judgment is usually on a subjective, emotional plane rather than an analytical one.

One favorite dogma of the "expert" is that there should be no indentations in the exterior walls, particularly at the corners. The farmer who built the first four-cornered barn had a legitimate objective, but his plan does not have to serve as the model for every dwelling house. Corners have been a challenge to architects for centuries, for the shadows and planes created at a corner or at an entrance can lend character, expression, and interest to an entire house.

So if, for example, your architect comes up with a solution something like this,

EXAMPLE A

don't be too quick to fill in all the corners. The problem is more complex than simply getting the maximum square footage under a given roof.

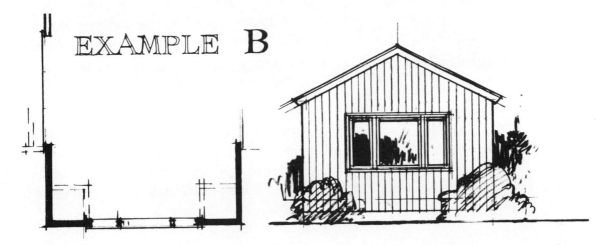

Though a few additional square feet of living space are gained by squaring off the corners, it is at the sacrifice of shadow, form, mass, and character.

Guesstimates

The projected cost of the house at this stage is, frankly, guesswork, but an architect, by the terms of the contract, is bound to submit a "statement of probable cost." Usually a "ball-park" figure is discussed, arrived at by using rule-of-thumb square-foot costs. This figure is very unreliable, however, and no realistic estimate can be made without more information. The architect must make the best assessment that he can, and how much faith you place in it is largely a question of how much you trust your architect's experience with this type of construction and his batting average with respect to budgets. Some architects are consistently unrealistic regarding costs. Presumably you inquired about this when the architect was selected, so now is the time to show some faith. A quick budget estimate based on the drawings and a tentative list of materials might be made by a builder at this point, but even this is bound to be general.

Though no guarantees can be made, the architect is clearly obligated morally and professionally to respect your goals, so he should be realistic with respect to probable costs. You are, of course, under the same obligation to be realistic and frank with the architect as this is the only way to avoid one of the most common misunderstandings between architects and their clients.

At this point, the architect has completed 15 percent of his services and is entitled to 15 percent of his estimated fee. In the event that you and your architect now part company, his estimated fee could be appropriately set at 15 percent of the budgeted building cost. Or you may have agreed on a lump sum that is independent of the building's projected cost. (Usually 5 percent of this projected fee would have been paid "on account" at the signing of the owner/architect agreement, and only the balance of 10 percent would be due now.)

When a misunderstanding arises between architect and client, it is often at the schematic design stage, particularly if the client changes his mind and decides not to go ahead for one reason or another. The fee is still due to the architect even if the client does not like the solution or feels he has no further use for the drawings. This is why it is terribly important to investigate your architect very carefully before hiring him, not just in terms of his success in acquiring clients, but in his demonstrated ability to understand his clients' goals and to refrain from subordinating them to his own stylistic predilections.

In most cases, fortunately, the clients are pleased with what they see and decide to proceed with the next stage. But whatever reservations they have should be expressed in a letter that should be acknowledged in writing by the architect as a double check against any misunderstandings. Upon receipt of his incremental fee and the "go ahead" from the owner, the architect begins the next phase—that of design development. This will comprise another 20 percent of his services; hence, when this phase is completed, another 20 percent of his total fee will be due.

DESIGN DEVELOPMENT PHASE

The schematic design was largely conceptual in character, illustrated by impressionistic sketches and perhaps study models. Now the design must be "hard-lined"; that is, the architect must come to terms with such things as the mechanics of heating and cooling, window types, and a basic structural system. Though this phase is still largely the domain of the architect, he will begin to involve you, his client, in decisions regarding kitchen layouts, window and door locations, various furniture arrangements, and possible finish materials. You may tend to get very specific and emphasize your taste for such things as hand-split shingles and fieldstone fireplaces. But many a successful house has been built with composition roofing and stuccoed concrete block without offending the owner's aesthetic sensibilities, while making the impact on the bank account far less traumatic. Until you know how the budget costs are going to develop, discuss the options and priorities with the architect, but stay flexible and hold whatever decisions you can in abeyance.

It is generally extremely helpful to involve a builder as cost consultant at this stage. A builder is often willing to confer with an owner and an architect as a courtesy, but this involves a considerable amount of work for him and there is then an implied obligation to engage him for the actual construction. Unless you have already selected your contractor, it is better to pay the builder a fee for this service—perhaps at his standard hourly rate. You should pay this fee directly to the contractor, after it has been approved by the architect. An architect, as a professional, should not be in the position of paying money directly to a contractor.

The budget is usually a matter of considerable concern, so these meetings should be devoted to planning the meshing of the various elements of the design so that everything "works" within the assigned budget. If this proves to be impossible, then your budget is unrealistic, and it is far better to discover this now than to run into considerable grief later on. Time and money invested at this preliminary stage should result in a substantial saving in the final cost of the house.

Preliminaries

The "prelims" consist of drawings of the projected house, both inside and out, together with detailed floor and site plans. They are the culmination of the developed design phase and should accomplish two goals. First, they should be sufficiently graphic to show you, the client, exactly what the design offers in terms of its floor plan, its proportions both in elevation and cross section, and its general character and appearance. The prelims are pictorial, not technical, drawings, though key dimensions are indicated. The floor plans, in particular, should be very clear and legible, showing furniture drawn to scale so you can imagine yourself in the house. Supplementary perspective sketches are made to illustrate features in each room, enabling you to understand the design. You are entitled to receive whatever drawings or study models you may need to help you visualize what the architect has in mind.

The second function of the prelims is to provide a builder with sufficient information to enable him to estimate the cost of the "basic shell" of the house with a fairly high degree of accuracy. The basic shell includes the foundations (perhaps exclusive of the chimney), the framing complete with roof decks and the plywood sheathing that goes under the siding, and the outside "skin"—that is, the siding and the roofing. You might wish to request prices for various alternate roofing and siding materials to get a clear picture of the available options.

The prelims are often the key drawings which will be expanded into subsequent, more detailed working drawings. They include the site plan, floor plans, sections, and elevations, but not construction details. They are made on tracing paper, and inexpensive copies can be made at any stage. Progress prints are periodically made for review, and more often than not they become covered with notes, "thumbnail" sketches, and various illegible scribbles. But they are apt to be important documents and should be selectively preserved as memoranda of meetings.

Preliminaries usually resemble schematics in format, but they are more thoroughly developed and refined and are usually executed with a greater sense of commitment. The site plan suggests all kinds of possibilities for site development and land use; the floor plans, usually drawn to a scale of $\frac{1}{4}$ of an inch per foot, show furniture layouts in considerable detail; the location of all built-in cabinets, cupboards, and bookcases; kitchen layouts; and the character and extent of the landscaping around the house. The sections and elevations are more highly detailed than before and should be helpful in showing you what form the building has taken, they also give the builder an idea of the quantities and shapes he will be dealing with.

A perspective drawing or two, showing what the building will actually look like from a given viewpoint, is usually part of the pre-liminaries. A "bird's-eye" perspective is sometimes included to illustrate the relationship between the various parts of the proposed house and its overall sculptural quality. Each architect has his own favorite technique for doing perspectives—pencil, pen and ink, watercolor, colored pencil. Communication is the principal purpose of these sketches; they are not a marketing device to sell an idea.

It is important to understand that perspectives at this stage are not just freehand approximations of what a building will look like from a given position. They are actually "constructed" using the principles of descriptive geometry, and they are technically accurate. The proportions in these drawings are not the result of the designer's wishful thinking or artistic license.

It is not necessary at this phase to make a final decision about fenestration—the window and door types and sizes. There is a substantial difference in cost between budget-line aluminum sliding glass doors and wooden French doors, with appropriate hardware, saddles, and finishing. The same is true of casement windows (the kind that swing out) as opposed to double-hung windows (the kind that slide up and down), which tend to be considerably less expensive. But to develop a realistic budget estimate, some guidelines or general descriptions of such basic components as the heating system must be outlined so that an approximation of cost can be estimated for each principal subcontractor.

Outline Specifications

An "outline spec" is either typed and bound into an 8½-by-11-inch binder, or indicated directly on the preliminary drawings. It includes a brief description of the volume of work allotted to each of the various trades, sufficiently detailed to enable a subcontractor to have a pretty good idea of what is expected. It also gives you an opportunity to review the basis for the estimate and to be sure you and the architect have been talking about the same thing.

This type of specification is really a list of materials rather than a description of how they are to be installed, and serves as a checklist to be sure that all cost categories are covered in determining the final budget estimate.

86

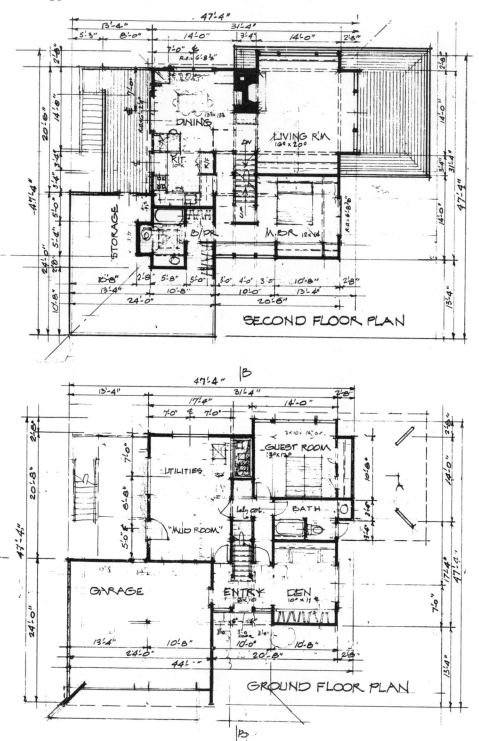

SECOND FLOOR PLAN

GROUND FLOOR PLAN

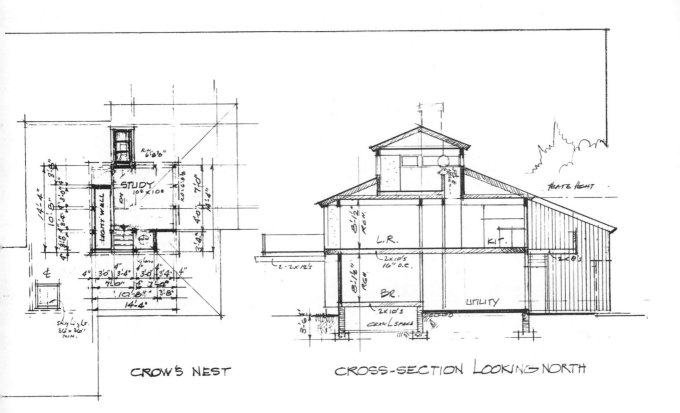

CROW'S NEST

CROSS-SECTION LOOKING NORTH

THE BUSHFIELD HOUSE—DEVELOPED DESIGN PHASE. The *"preliminaries" of the Bushfield residence, with more complete dimensioning than in the schematics and more information provided for budget estimates of the house's component parts.*

PLOT PLAN

A HOUSE FOR
MRS HAMILTON BASSO
MANICE & BAKER , ARCHITECTS , NEW YORK , N.Y

A HOUSE FOR
MR & MRS DOUGLAS D. SCHOULER , POUND RIDGE , N.Y.
MANICE & BAKER , ARCHITECTS , 342 MADISON AVE , N.Y.C.

PHASE I   VIEW FROM NORTH EAST

BAKER RESIDENCE , GIRDLE RIDGE ROAD, KATONAH N.Y.
PHASE I   JOHN MILNES BAKER A.I.A   ARCHITECT , N.Y. N.Y.

RENDERINGS. *The preliminary drawings usually include one or more renderings in perspective, using descriptive geometry techniques to ensure accuracy as a final indication of what the client can expect in reality.*

A HOUSE FOR
MR & MRS JOHN MILNES BAKER (AND IAN, JENNIFER, & JAMIE BAKER)
GIRDLE RIDGE ROAD, KATONAH, N.Y.   John Milnes Baker ARCH'T
PHASE II

J.M. BAKER HOUSES INC   John Milton Baker A.I.A.

This is one of a series of stock plans available to builders and developers through J. M. BAKER HOUSES Inc., a builder support program developed by the author. The portfolio includes numerous designs addressing a variety of typical family needs. These plans can be easily modified to incorporate specific requirements of individual buyers.

This particular house was developed for a site where the main approach is possible only from the south. It is desirable to have the rooms face the sun and view over the driveway. The ground floor has therefore been elevated at least four feet above the level of the driveway. The view from the living room, dining room, and kitchen is above the tops of the cars parked in front of the house. Even a

(Other house plans from this series are shown on pages 77, 92, 93, and 94-95.)

terrace or garden can be developed between the house and the driveway. A low hedge on top of a three-foot-high retaining wall would assure an attractive and private space.

VIEW OF DINING ROOM INGLENOOK

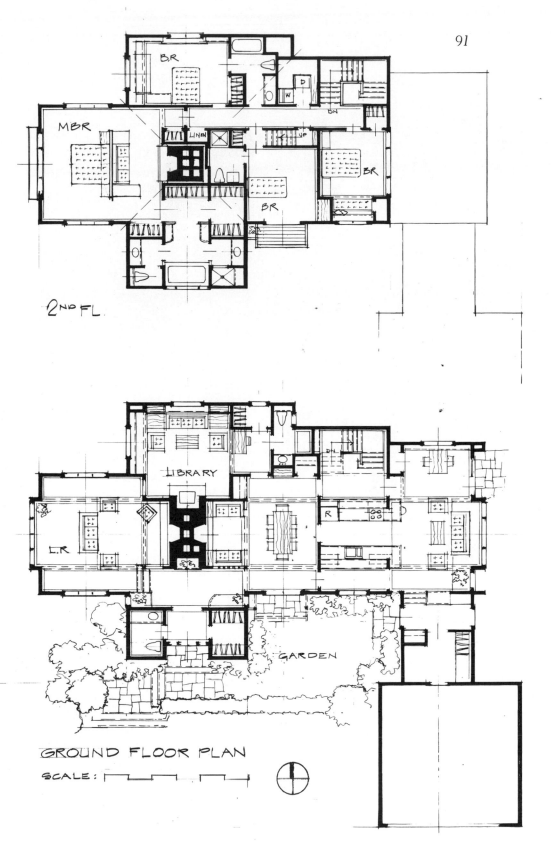

BR

MBR

LINEN

BR

BR

W

DN

UP

2ND FL.

LIBRARY

L.R

R

DN

GARDEN

GROUND FLOOR PLAN

SCALE:

A HOUSE FOR

MR & MRS STUART ELDERKIN, VALPARAISO, INDIANA

John Nichols Baker A.I.A.

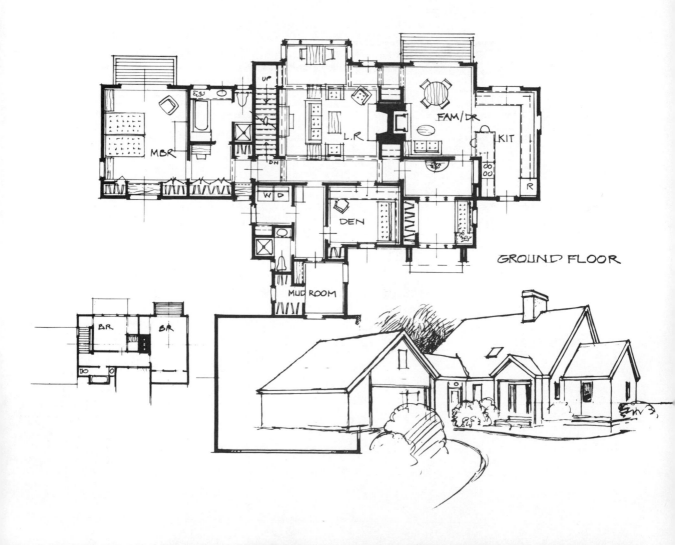

MBR

L.R

FAM/DR

KIT

R

WD

DEN

UP

DN

MUD ROOM

GROUND FLOOR

BR.

BR.

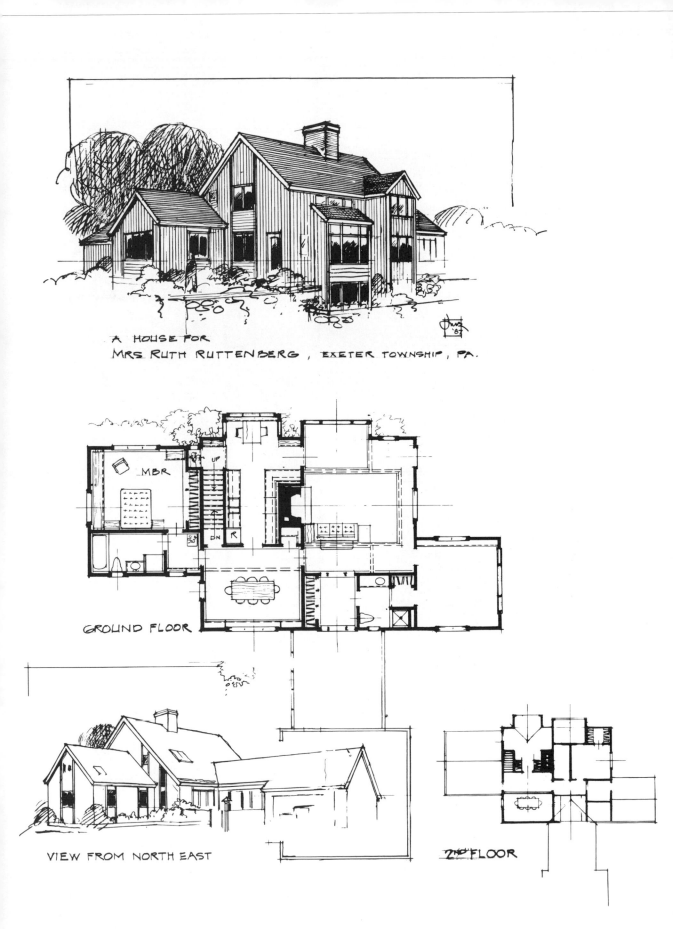

A HOUSE FOR
MRS RUTH RUTTENBERG, EXETER TOWNSHIP, PA.

MBR

UP

DN   R

GROUND FLOOR

VIEW FROM NORTH EAST

2ND FLOOR

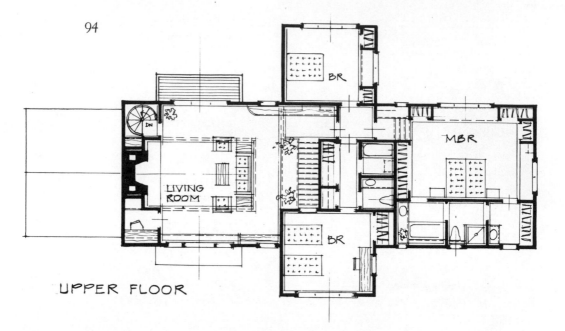

UPPER FLOOR

The living room is on the upper level of this house. With or without a spectacular view, the elevated space offers a wonderful sense of privacy that has considerable appeal.

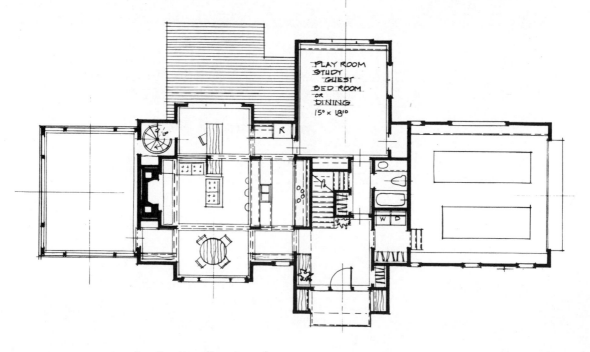

SCALE: 0' 4' 8' 12' 16' 20'

GROUND FLOOR

A HOUSE FOR
J. M. BAKER ASSOCIATES Ltd, OLD POST ROAD, POUND RIDGE, N.Y.

This house is part of the
J. M. BAKER HOUSES Inc.
series of stock plans
available to franchised
builders and developers.
(See page 90.)

INGLENOOK

FAMILY ROOM / DINING

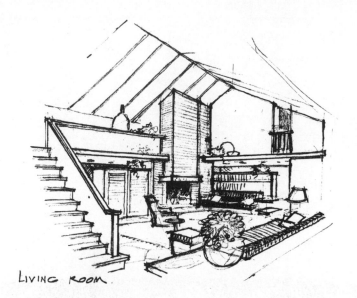

LIVING ROOM.

Interior sketches used to give the owners a "feel" for what the inside of the house might be like.

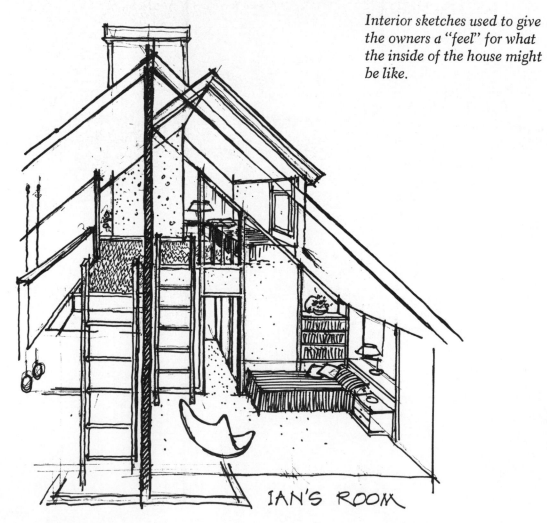

IAN'S ROOM

Budget Estimate

The budget estimate provides the basis for the architect's "statement of probable construction cost," which is required by his legal contract with the owner. Sufficient information was shown on the preliminary drawings to allow the builder to make a "quantity take-off" of all the major elements of the basic shell, and the outline specification gave a general description of the remaining components.

Allowances can be included for kitchen cabinets, the well, the sewage system, all based on an experienced familiarity with the various aspects of the job. Not every single item can be priced at this point and assumptions must still be made, but the margin of error is greatly reduced.

At this point, with the firm cost of the basic shell and the approximate unit costs for finishing materials and various trades established, you will, for the first time, have a good idea how much of your budget is left for millwork (any prefabricated wooden feature such as stairs and cabinets) and finishes. If compromises must be made, priority can be established and the options clearly presented.

Upon presentation of the developed design drawings and a statement of probable cost in line with the anticipated budget, the architect has completed this phase of his services and is entitled to a total of 35 percent of his anticipated fee. He should not start work on the next phase until he has been paid. If the architect's statement of probable construction cost is in excess of your assigned budget, the architect should make whatever recommendations and revisions are required to meet the budget at no additional charge. If, however, you suddenly have second thoughts about spending so much and decide to greatly reduce the scope of the project, the changes in the design constitute a change in program and the architect's fee must increase to cover the extra work.

CONSTRUCTION DOCUMENTS

The construction documents consist of working drawings, specifications, general conditions, special conditions, and addenda. The preliminary drawings gave a vivid and quite detailed impression of the house. They are not detailed enough for a builder to work from, however, and before construction can begin, complete dimensional drawings must be made of every component of the house. There should be sufficient detail to ensure that the various elements will fit neatly together and that the contractor's final estimate of the cost of construction will be accurate.

These are the "working drawings," and they are complemented by a bound set of specifications listing the various items to be used in the building and indicating precisely how they are to be fitted together.

The drawings and specs are mutually supportive, and together they provide the single most valuable bulwark against misunderstandings with the builder. Elements that can best be communicated graphically are shown in the drawings, and those that can be most precisely delineated verbally are listed in the specifications; the two work together to ensure the construction of a harmonious house.

Working Drawings (Blueprints)

The developed design drawings, or prelims, were previously described as a skeleton set of working drawings. Assuming that no substantial changes were ordered after the receipt of the budget estimates, these prelims are simply further amplified, refined, and modified to describe in as much detail as necessary every item in the house.

Working drawings are scale drawings made on tracing paper. The reproductions of these tracings are often called blueprints. They used to be white-line prints on blue paper (hence the name), but nowadays they are more often black- or blue-line positives on white paper.

Though you are entitled to a set for your own use, the tracings (the originals) and the prints used by the builder actually remain the property of the architect. They are "instruments of service" and not a commodity which you can purchase. This is one of the means by which the architect protects his design from plagiarism.

In addition to the construction drawings, known as architectural drawings, there are usually separate drawings, called the mechanical sheets, for electrical work, plumbing, and "H.V.A.C." (Heating, Ventilating, Air Conditioning, and Cooling).

Before the prelims have been embellished with dimension lines, sepia transparencies are made from the original tracings. The sepias, which can be drawn on and later printed as separate drawings, are ideal for duplicate plans which can be annotated for each trade or subcontractor. The architectural drawings get so filled up with notes, lines, and symbols that they sometimes become almost illegible with too much information crammed into one drawing.

The development of quick reproduction machines has made it easy to copy the details and schedules on 8½-by-11-inch sheets. They are easy to refer to if kept together in a binder-back notebook or on a clipboard. Drawings on a job site have a way of getting very messy and hard to read (often even hard to find, after a while). Detailed drawings on 8½-by-11-inch sheets can be clipped to a board or tacked up as specific reference sheets for particular jobs—for example, closet shelving—along with any instruction sheets and supplementary drawings issued during the course of construction.

With the drawings the architect provides schedules of finishes, hardware, and door and window types, listing the quantity and location of each of the various items. In residential work, it is often more convenient to prepare these schedules on 8½-by-11-inch sheets and keep them with the instruction sheets and specs in a notebook or on a clipboard.

Clients often think that working drawings are merely technical translations of design drawings, but this is definitely not the case. They are creative efforts in themselves and thought, sensitivity, and imagination are required to develop a set of working drawings. This process cannot be left to the builder for there are design decisions that have to be made at virtually every step along the way. A clumsy or heavy-handed detail can ruin a good design. If, for example, a windowsill is placed 36 inches above the floor instead of 30, the view from a living-room chair might be restricted just enough to detract from a fuller enjoyment of the room—and the view. Too steep a pitch to the run of stairs, ill-matched proportions of windows to doors, and countless other seemingly minor details can have a similar effect. There are literally innumerable design decisions, often of a subtle nature, that are made during the working drawing stage. If care is not taken over details, even a well-planned house will lose the special quality that makes a space seem to respond sympathetically to the mood and spirit of the people in it.

Paul Coker, Jr., presented the author with this cartoon when his house was completed. He elected to change from French doors to sliding glass doors during the construction of the house (see page 170).

I once visited an attractive contemporary house that had one curiously incongruous feature. All the doors in the living room were 8 feet tall, even the 2-foot-wide closet doors to the bar. Their proportions were distorted in relation to the average size of a human being. The owners apparently kept the room as a "parlor" for guests and rarely used it by themselves. I suspect that the proportions of the doors alone could well have introduced a disquieting, subconscious fear that a 7-foot-tall creature with long, skinny arms and fingers might jump through the opening some dark night. The doors had such freakish proportions that they had the same disquieting effect as crazy mirrors in a carnival fun house. The scale of the room could easily have been reduced to that of the normal human being by using standard doors and by emphasizing the horizontality of the wall at a 6-foot-8-inch or 7-foot level.

The moment has now arrived when you must come to a final decision about the details of doors, windows, and finishes, and the location of the electrical outlets and kitchen fixtures. Louvered doors cost more than flush ones; built-in bathroom counters with integrally molded basins are not bought for the same price as a simple lavatory. So be careful and don't keep coming back to your architect with last-minute inspirations and discoveries unless you are prepared to pay the price in terms of time and money.

Paul Coker, Jr.'s Connecticut house was completely enclosed and the French doors installed when he opted for sliding glass doors after all. The change order was executed, the doors ordered, and the progress of the work interrupted for several weeks. The picture the owner gave me (opposite) attests to his sense of humor as well as his acknowledgment of his responsibility for the costly change in design.

Particular attention should be paid to the electrical plans and the kitchen layout. For some reason, clients often resist focusing their attention on electrical layouts. More last-minute changes are made in the lighting design during construction than in any other area. If the symbols and conventions used to identify the various outlets, switches, and electrical devices seem confusing, it is only because they are unfamiliar, not because they are complicated. The most common ones are illustrated on page 103, and a schedule of typical fixtures is shown. You should start thinking about the electrical plan at the developed design stage, when the architect is producing the prelims, so that a tentative layout can be indicated and the budget estimated. Often the architect will make a sepia of the ¼-inch-scale preliminary drawing and draw in the probable furniture layouts with symbols for about 90 percent of the electrical switches, outlets, and fixtures. The remaining 10 percent is your responsibility as the client.

When working on the electrical plan of your house, concentrate on one room at a time. Remember that every outlet, switch, and fixture location costs around $25, apart from the cost of the fixture, and they add up quickly. To change them later costs a lot more, so go over every room carefully, and don't forget to consider the exterior lighting. Keep your questions for a final session with your architect. It is usually a good idea to go through each room (and the exterior) to check all the symbols with the architect once the basic shell of the house has been completed. Indicate with a crayon or Magic Marker the precise location on the studs of any special fixtures and the average height of wall plugs.

There are two methods of covering the cost of fixtures when drawing up the contract. One is by means of an allowance. If the final selection exceeds the allowance, you pay the difference; if there is a saving, it is credited to you. The other method is to leave the fixtures out of the contract completely. You may supply some items yourself; or the architect may purchase them for you at his discount rate, but you must reimburse him and pay him an additional 15 percent markup for his overhead.

Specifications

The final specifications are written descriptions of all the materials, equipment, and component parts which go to make up the house and of the responsibilities of every contractor and subcontractor involved in the job and all vendors supplying materials. Specs must complement the working drawings in every detail. A clear set of specifications is as effective a device as any in assuring quality construction.

When preparing the specifications and working drawings the architect is faced with a dilemma that is particularly acute in residential work. These documents will, in all probability, be submitted to several builders who will use them as a basis when estimating their bids for the job. Once a bid has been accepted, the builder is legally obligated to construct the house, as outlined in the specifications and working draw-

ELECTRIC SYMBOLS

SWITCHES

- ⌇ SWITCH
- ⌇ᴰ SWITCH w/DIMMER
- ⌇³ 3-WAY SWITCH
- ⌇○ SWITCH & OUTLET

OUTLETS

- ⊖ DUPLEX OUTLET
- ⊖ᵂᴼ WATERPROOF
- ⬤ ½ SWITCHED
- ⊘ SPECIAL PURPOSE
- ⊖ᴿ RANGE
- ⊖ᵂ WASHER
- ⊖ᴰ DRYER
- ⊙ FLOOR

FIXTURES

- ⊗ CEILING
- ⊠ ⊗ RECESSED
- ⊢⊗ BRACKET
- ⌄⊗ FAN
- ⊗━━━━ TRACK
- ⊨══⊨ FLUORESCENT

MISCELLANEOUS

- ▭ PANEL   ◀ TELEPHONE
- ▽ BUZZER   ◁J JACK
- ▭▷ BELL   ◇ INT. COM

NOTE: ALWAYS SPECIFY COLOR OF OUTLET OR SWITCH

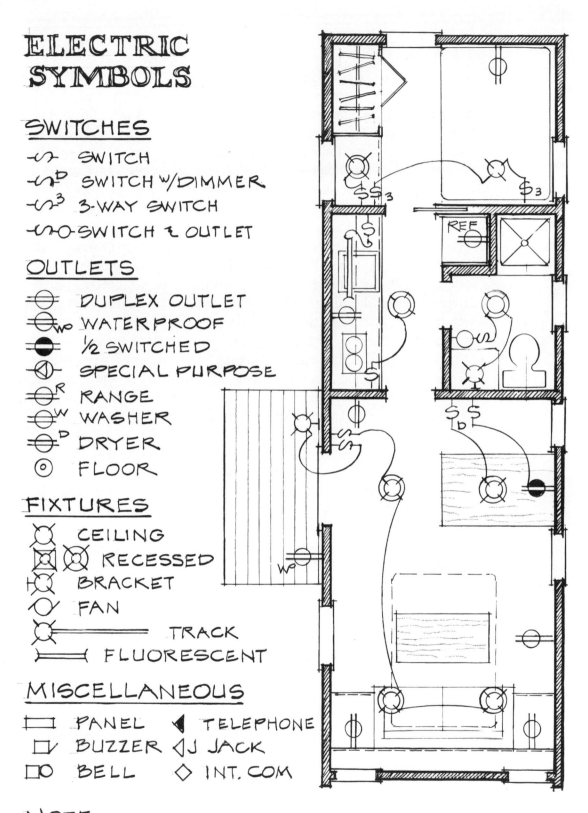

ings, for the bid price. If the specs and working drawings are too elaborate and minutely detailed, the builders will take fright and prices will be high. If, on the other hand, they are too skimpy, this will lead to challenge and debate later on, and a low initial bid may well be followed by innumerable requests for extras. Inadequate information will lead to misunderstandings, but redundant verbiage is confusing and unnecessary.

If the contractors bidding or negotiating the job are carefully selected by you and the architect for their reliability and competence, "long-form" specifications are not necessary. Under these circumstances specs should be simply a clear list of components with a general inclusive statement regarding the scope of the work and the quality of performance. No one wants the building process to be a nit-picking game of semantics, and builders abhor extras even more than an owner or architect, because their time schedules can be completely disrupted by changes in the scope of the work during the construction phase.

Wherever possible a virtual shopping list of required items should be made out, with manufacturer's name, catalog number, and type, size, and color. This policy applies particularly to such things as windows, plumbing fixtures and accessories, and any other stock items of whatever sort.

Specifications are divided into sections by trade, roughly approximating the order in which the trades become involved in the building process. The first section is usually general and is applicable to all the trade sections. It covers such things as insurance requirements, safety precautions, and general liability, and it invariably refers to A.I.A. Document A201, "General Conditions of the Contract for Construction."

This document has been periodically revised since 1911, and includes articles covering almost every aspect of the construction phase. The current edition includes the following Table of Articles:

Contract Documents
Architect
Owner
Contractor
Subcontractors
Separate Contracts
Miscellaneous Provisions
Time
Payments and Completion

Protection of Persons and Property
Insurance
Changes in the Work
Uncovering and Correction of Work
Termination of the Contract

Though the highlights of these articles are discussed in this text, you should obtain a copy of this document from your architect, your local chapter of the American Institute of Architects, or the American Institute of Architects (1735 New York Avenue, N.W., Washington, D.C. 20006). Study it carefully. To use its own words: "This Document has important legal consequences; consultation with an attorney is encouraged with respect to its modification." It has been approved and endorsed by the Associated General Contractors of America.

After the preliminary general section the subsequent sections of the specification booklet cover all the trades involved. (See the requisition on the Smith house on page 122 for a typical list of trades.) The site work section, for example, should be explicit as to who does what. What happens to the trees that are cut down and what about the stumps? Does the contractor who does the clearing and the excavation also trench for the utility lines? Or do the electrical contractor and the plumbing contractor do their own excavation?

Specs for "Masonry and Concrete" usually follow next, then for "Carpentry" and "Millwork." I usually expand the section on millwork to include "Accessories," which then becomes the shopping list for items that are purchased by the general contractor and installed according to the specifications for carpentry.

Addenda

If supplementary information or corrections are added to the specifications, an addendum (or addenda) is issued. If, for example, drawings have been issued for bids, and a contractor calls in with a question because of an ambiguity, an addendum is issued, not only to him, but to all the other contractors and to anyone who received an original copy. Addenda have a way of getting lost, so a complete record of them should be maintained and copies of the transmittal forms kept in the architect's files. In formal bidding procedures receipts should be obtained for each addendum that is issued.

Consultants

On occasion either the owner or the architect may want to involve outside consultants, who bring a depth of knowledge in their own field to the project that the architect is not expected to have. The professionals most often consulted in residential work are the interior designer, the landscape architect, and solar engineers, though acoustical consultants and electronic advisers are sometimes involved. A kitchen planner can also be consulted, in which case he should be given complete responsibility for purchasing and coordinating the installation of all kitchen equipment. Under normal circumstances these specialists are actually retained by the owner; if hired by the architect, their fees are a reimbursable expense.

If you intend to employ a landscape architect or interior designer, it is best to make your selection at the very outset of the project, with the architect's approval because they will have to work very closely together. In this way the specialized expertise of these professionals can benefit the project from the beginning.

A landscape architect, for example, can be helpful in selecting one site over another. If the interior designer understands the architect's goals, the integration of color, texture, and wood can be incorporated in the design when the prelims are being drawn up, or at the latest during the construction document phase. Each consultant has a role to play, and as a professional, each understands the value of an integrated and harmonious design.

Interior Designer

Interior designers have valuable special knowledge of colors, textures, and fabrics. They are also familiar with the best sources for various interior furnishings. Many projects benefit from their sensitive reflection and professional advice. Some designers, however, impose their own personal style on the furnishings whether or not it is appropriate for a particular house. (Some architects have the same affliction!) A good professional designer has much in common with a good theatrical director, who subordinates the projection of his or her own personality to the total impact of the play. In both cases the maturity and skill of the professional in charge produce a spontaneous effect.

Unfortunately, often the interior designer is not involved in the project from the beginning but, instead, is called in to "decorate" when the architect has already completed the house. This may have worked in the days when building styles were more standardized and less innovative, but in contemporary architecture so many textures and built-in furnishings are part of the building itself that it is almost essential for the interior consultant to be part of the design team from the beginning, so that the architect and designer can work together to achieve an integrated whole for their client.

Landscape Architect

It is unusual for a client to retain the services of a licensed professional landscape architect. Most clients call on the local nurseryman to assist them in selecting shrubbery and trees that will grow well and complement the house as the years go by. Nurserymen can be extremely helpful as consultants. With the trend toward more naturalistic landscaping with indigenous species, the nurseryman's local knowledge can be of tremendous value. This works particularly well if the architect has a feeling for landscape design and can provide a master plan for the nurseryman to follow.

The advantage of employing a landscape architect is that he is trained to think of outside spaces in relation to a wide range of visual and spatial experiences. Without disparaging or deprecating the imagination or skill of a good nurseryman, he does not bring to the site the architectonic discipline that the professional landscape architect can; the landscape architect's sense of scale, of spatial modulation, and of dramatic effect can complement the architectural work by extending the total design far beyond the house's foundation.

With the completion of the contract documents—that is, the working drawings and the specifications—the project enters its final phase. When the architect has completed the design development stage, 40 percent of his fee is due him for his services on this phase of the work. The architect will have received at this stage 75 percent of his total fee, and another 5 percent is due when the owner/contractor agreement is resolved, as the project enters its final phase.

"Brains first and then Hard Work. . . . That's the way to build a house," said Eeyore.

A. A. Milne,
The House at Pooh Corner

3 THE IMPLEMENTATION
Construction–The Builder's Domain

The construction phase of a house can be the exciting culmination of months of planning and design, or it can be a nightmare of frustrating crises. If a sympathetic and mutually respectful relationship has developed between you, the architect, and the contractor, the actual building of the house will be fun and exciting. Even though many of the component parts of a house are mass produced, the process of putting these parts together is a craft requiring great skill, subject to the human limitations and imperfections that give each project its own individuality. The knots in a pine board may infuse that wood with a pattern and variety which make it infinitely more appealing than the perfect regularity of a board with uniform grain. If a builder brings craftsmanship and skill to his work and the momentum and enthusiasm of all concerned are sustained, the execution of each detail will contribute to the quality of the whole.

The construction phase of a house begins once a builder has been selected and the agreement between him and you, the owner, signed. Though you and the architect will stay involved throughout, it is the builder who now plays the leading role. It is his expertise, his efficiency, and his attitude which make this phase run smoothly. Consequently, it is important to understand and appreciate what builders do and what criteria should be employed in their selection.

BUILDING CONTRACTORS

The general contractor coordinates the various phases of the work and supervises the construction crew. He is responsible for the entire production of the building. He is paid a fee to cover his overhead costs and provide his profit. The amount varies, but it is usually approximately 15 percent of the basic cost of the work. The cost of the work is the amount of money the contractor pays out for services, materials, and wages paid to employees working directly on a specific job (but not to office personnel whose wages come under overhead).

For his fee the contractor organizes the entire construction of the house, supervising the work of all the subcontractors and seeing that everything happens when it should and that the work is done properly, in strict accordance with the drawings and specifications and follows the best customary practice in the various trades. Trying to put together all the various aspects of a building operation into a harmonious whole is a time-consuming and, at times, frustrating procedure and requires a firm and knowledgeable person with executive ability. A contractor who makes things run smoothly earns every penny of his fee.

In residential work there are apt to be two types of builders: the carpenter-builder who actually works on the job himself as the field foreman, and does his office work at home, and the construction company. There are advantages to each, and which type to employ depends upon the complexity of the project, the calendar, and the local situation.

Carpenter-Builders

The carpenter-builder is usually a craftsman who enjoys working with his hands and, because he is his own boss and directly responsible to you and the architect, his workmanship is often excellent. The carpenter-builder is not always a business executive, so his paperwork sometimes suffers. For alteration work or for a new house under about 2,500 square feet (a three- or four-bedroom house with a living room, dining room, family room, and kitchen), the carpenter-builder is normally the better choice.

If you enjoy a certain amount of involvement with the job, you can establish a closer relationship with this kind of builder than with a construction company. His overhead costs are usually lower than those of the construction company, so you may benefit from this saving as long as he devotes his full time and attention to your job. On the other hand, if the job drags for any reason and the carpenter-builder gets nervous about his profit margin, prospective work may become more important to him than the job under construction. It is an infuriating and frustrating experience to arrive at a job and find no one there.

A builder once confided in me that while finishing a job he managed to keep his next customer at bay for at least a week by depositing on the job site some sawhorses, a few old planks, and a broken cement mixer.

When interviewing a prospective builder, therefore, it is very important to discuss continuity and momentum. You should also check with his previous customers as to how conscientiously he followed through, particularly at the last stages of a job. As any job can go sour for a number of reasons, it is not fair to judge a builder negatively from one or two reports; get a general consensus of his customers and the architects he has worked for.

Construction Companies

For complex work involving considerable coordination of the various trades, the construction company is probably a better choice than the carpenter-builder. Whereas a carpenter-builder can usually take on only one house at a time, the larger organization, with its office staff, can handle several jobs concurrently. Often there is an overlapping of subcontractors from one job to another, and the increased communication between them and the general contractor benefits all the owners. It is the function of the construction company to see that the job runs smoothly and efficiently—it's the only way the company can get more work.

Usually the more complex the job, and the longer it takes to complete, the less direct contact you will have with the builder. The architect is the liaison between the company and you, making the relationship with the company more formal than with the carpenter-builder. If the construction company specializes in residential work—particularly where architects are involved—the cost of employing a company need not be any higher than using a carpenter-builder. The more objective, formal relationship is sometimes conducive to a more productive, efficient building process.

Which way to go, then, depends on the complexity of the job, your temperament, and, to a lesser extent, on finances, though I must re-emphasize that the carpenter-builder will not necessarily cost less. In the final analysis the confidence a particular builder inspires, his availability, and the architect's assessment will tilt the balance one way or the other.

When searching for the right builder, you and the architect should keep your list of candidates relatively short, limiting it to three or four whom you two will interview in depth and from whom you will request estimates. All these contractors should be in the same category and enjoy the reputation of being quality builders. It is unrealistic to compare bids from an experienced, established firm accustomed to working with architects with those from a jobber builder who operates out of the cab of his truck. The risks you run in selecting the latter may not warrant accepting what at first appears to be a lower price. There is much more to building a house than the layman can imagine, and many a competent carpenter has failed as a builder because of complexities he couldn't handle. So don't be wooed by the inexperienced unless you are aware of the potential hazards and are prepared to take a gamble.

Owner as General Contractor

Since the general contractor's role is essentially one of coordination and supervision, occasionally an owner who has some knowledge of building—usually not as much as he thinks—decides to act as his own general contractor and save the 15 percent which would usually go on the contractor's fee. Subcontractors, and even vendors, usually will not figure the same amount for a job if they are dealing with an owner who, as an amateur, is likely to waste a lot of their time asking questions before coming to a decision and who cannot be counted on for repeat work over the years. Thus the apparent 15 percent saving is often eliminated by the increase in the subcontractors' fees.

Construction Manager

The so-called "CM" approach offers an alternative to either employing a general contractor or filling his role yourself. It is relatively new but increasingly popular in the commercial and institutional fields. It also has advantages in residential work.

A construction manager is an owner's agent, experienced in all phases of construction, hired to coordinate and administer the actual building of the house. He differs from a general contractor in that he works on a professional fee basis and is solely responsible for protecting your interests and saving you money wherever possible. He authorizes all payments, which you then must pay directly.

The construction manager is brought in as soon as you approve the parti, at the schematic design phase of a project, and he acts as a cost consultant throughout the job. He obtains comparative estimates from the principal subcontractors at each successive stage and negotiates the final contracts between you and the subcontractors, much as a general contractor does when "shopping" for his prices on a competitive bid basis. Sometimes the construction manager is a general contractor who is willing to work for a flat fee or on a salary basis. The fixed amount eliminates any suggestion that the manager has an incentive to drag the job along.

Another possibility is to hire your architect to act as construction manager. The responsibility is, of course, in addition to his role under the standard services contract and his fee will increase. Because he is already responsible for administering the construction contract, his fee will be less than the 15 percent a contractor would charge, and if he will undertake the work, you should save at least 5 percent of the construction cost.

If this method is adopted, the work can be separated into four basic categories: site work, masonry, mechanical work (plumbing, heating, and electrical), and carpentry. The carpentry contractor takes on the role of job foreman, and the architect-construction manager that of executive coordinator, purchaser, and superintendent. Each of the subcontractors and the owner must carry liability insurance and workman's compensation. I built my own house this way, and far more time is involved than I had ever realized. So if you are thinking of hiring your architect as a construction manager, be sure your architect has done construction management work already and understands what is involved before he undertakes your project.

Another word of caution—the architect, particularly if he is young and inexperienced or temperamentally indecisive, may have difficulty organizing the "subs," who may have the same reservations they would have in working with an owner and inflate their cost figures proportionately. My advice is to use an architect-construction manager, like the carpenter-builder, only on projects under 2,500 square feet. This arrangement offers some savings, and the advantage of close and continuous involvement with the architect.

You should remember that the construction manager acts as your representative in dealing with all vendors and subcontractors, and his financial remuneration must be totally independent of the cost of the work. It is best established as a professional fee, independent of any fluctuations of the cost of the building. The "Standard Form of Agreement between Owner and Construction Manager" (A.I.A. Document B801) is the appropriate contract, and it outlines the terms and conditions of agreement. It is available from your architect, the local chapter of the American Institute of Architects (or the national office in Washington, D.C.).

BIDDING OR NEGOTIATION PHASE

When a construction project is submitted for bids, the understanding of what the builder is to do is based on the working drawings and specs, supplemented by any general and special conditions of the contract. The specifications, as already mentioned, should be clear without being overelaborate, and each set, of course, must be identical so that all contractors base their prices on the same set of requirements.

In the absence of a final decision on some specific item, such as a kitchen cabinet or a type of window, the maximum amount that can be spent on it must be clearly indicated. A reasonable approximation of the cost of such things as water supply, sewage disposal, and hardware can be estimated, and if the same allowance is carried by each builder, the comparison between their bids is fair and equitable. A builder's bid is submitted in the "Form of Proposal" prepared by the architect and completed by the contractors submitting bids (see page 120). When competitive prices are submitted by two or more bidders, certain formalities are followed, which your architect must observe.

Contracts

When selecting a builder, it is very important to have a clear, unambiguous contract. The contract is an agreement between a general contractor and you in which the contractor obligates himself to perform certain services in exchange for a remuneration. I shall confine myself here to a discussion of the standard forms of agreement commonly used in house construction.

Lump Sum

The lump-sum contract is best for simple, straightforward work without excessive details. In this type of contract the contractor or contractors submit a figure based on the final plans and specs. If the bid is high, he makes a profit; if it is low, he loses money.

The advantage of this type of bid is its simplicity; the disadvantage is that you never really know what his costs are or if he is paying an appropriate price, because the breakdown of costs is not submitted by the builder until he has been awarded the contract. This is fine as long as the low bid is within the budget, but if all the bids are too high, the common practice is to select the lowest bidder and negotiate with him. Considerable time can be wasted in this way and, if the bids are high and most of the special features of the house have to be sacrificed to the budget, these negotiations are a frustrating and discouraging experience which can dampen everyone's enthusiasm for the project.

Cost Plus

Under a cost-plus or time-and-materials ("T & M") contract, you pay a builder all his direct costs plus a fee of 10 to 20 percent. This is sometimes the only fair contract when there are extensive alterations or other work whose scope cannot be clearly defined. You obviously need to have confidence in the builder's integrity as well as in his skill.

In remodeling an old barn or house, where it is virtually impossible to predict whether the sills need replacing or how extensive the plumbing work will be, T & M is the only reasonable contract. If a builder is asked for a lump-sum figure on such work, or, for that matter, on new work with incomplete plans and specs, he will have to add a large contingency figure to cover any unforeseen costs. If the contingency turns out to be excessive, he pockets the difference by the nature of the lump-sum contract.

The T & M contract has the disadvantage of being open-ended with regard to cost. The final bill can be a horrendous shock even if a conscientious architect and contractor attempt to discipline the owner's enthusiasm for expanding the scope of the work as the project advances.

Upset Price

A third alternative, the "upset price" (a "not-to-exceed" amount), has distinct advantages for both the contractor and the owner. For example, the builder may agree to build a house for a sum not to exceed $200,000. He has based his price on the plans and specifications, including allowances for various items which are described in general terms but not specifically detailed. These allowances should be generous so that the owner knows what his "outside" price will be.

The builder is paid a fixed fee for his work, usually around 15 percent for his contractor's services, and the total contract amount includes his fixed fee. If the total cost of the work is less than the estimated amount, which often proves to be the case if the builder carefully executes details to conform to the specific allowances and gains time during construction so that his labor costs turn out to be lower than anticipated, the savings are divided equally between the owner and the builder. In effect, the only way the builder can increase his profit on the job is to save money for the owner.

Besides the advantage of knowing what the maximum cost will be, the upset-price contract offers you the possibility of saving time and a degree of flexibility that allows your ideas and the architect's refinements to be worked into the design during construction without the hassle of adjusting the lump-sum contract, or running the danger of a T & M job's getting out of hand. The monthly requisitions should be submitted in a breakdown of costs, called a "schedule of values," so that you, the architect, and the builder have a very clear financial picture as the job progresses.

Contract Procedures

The three types of contracts may appear in varied or combined forms. For example, the requisition for the Smith house on page 122 shows a lump-sum price on the basic shell of $55,000. The foundations, framing, siding, and roofing were all predictable costs, and the builder was selected on a competitive basis by bidding on this as a lump-sum amount. Because there were numerous unknowns at the time the owners wanted to start, allowances were made for *all* other items. Competitive prices were later obtained for each trade. This permitted the owners to feel secure about the fundamentals, but to explore various alternatives for each special element, such as bookcases, fencing, and floor finishes, with the selected contractor obtaining competitive bids from subcontractors.

Whatever contract form is used, do not under any circumstances proceed without a *written contract*. There is far too much at stake to chance proceeding on a handshake, or "gentleman's agreement." A gentleman should have no qualms whatsoever in legally binding himself by a fair and equitable contract.

I had the occasion to act as an expert witness for an owner in an arbitration case. The owner had commissioned a reputable architect to design a $45,000 house. The architect imaginatively solved the "problem," but permitted a builder to proceed on a good-faith letter, with no clear mutual understanding of the cost. The house ended up costing $90,000. In addition, the house had several construction defects, causing it to leak excessively. The architect claimed an increase in his fee for the increase in cost. As the builder, a carpenter-builder, died before the matter was resolved and the architect claimed his balances due, the poor owner was left with a leaky house and no recourse whatsoever. Had the budget been clearly established and the requisitions reviewed as the job progressed, something might have been done early in the project to protect this unfortunate owner from the shock of a 100 percent increase at the end of a job in which there had not been a single change order.

THE BUILDING OPERATION

Once the contract has been executed by both the builder and the owner, the work begins. Occasionally, when there is a pressing need to commence work, a builder may proceed with filing for permits, clearing the site, and "rough staking" the house upon the receipt of an owner's "letter of intent." But this is as far as he should be expected to go without a signed contract, and a specified *per diem* rate (plus expenses) should be authorized for this work in the event the project is aborted for any reason at the last minute.

A time period for construction is specified in the contract, and it is the builder's business to commence work as quickly as possible. He obtains the building permit from the local building department, usually by submitting two sets of final drawings with the architect's seal and the specifications and site plan survey. It usually takes a week or so for the building inspector to review the drawings and specifications and issue the permit.

Sometimes the architect, to be accommodating, will file for the permit and pay the permit fee. This fee is reimbursable to the architect by the owner unless the building contract has been signed, in which case the builder must reimburse the architect.

Getting Started

The house has been sited on the drawings, but it must be staked out precisely by the architect, although the builder usually supplies the stakes and a transit. If there is any question at this point as to the setback requirement—the minimum distance legally required by the local zoning ordinance between the house and all boundary lines of the property—a licensed surveyor should check the location *before* excavation begins. The mortgaging agencies usually require such a survey to ensure that the house is located within the setback requirements of the local building ordinances. (There have been instances where a house was started on the wrong lot!)

Don't be horrified by what appears to be the minuscule dimensions of your house at this stage. A string 18 or 20 feet stretched between stakes seems pretty short on the site, and a staked-out house invariably looks tiny. But don't worry: if it was right on paper, it will be right in actuality. A house tends to vary in size at different stages, and sometimes a client will practically panic about the seemingly inadequate dimensions. I even did so myself with my own house, particularly over the size of the living room. Fortunately, the rooms almost always end up the right size, and mine was no exception.

When trying to determine how long it will take to build your house, you should allow roughly a month of construction time for every $25,000 to $30,000 in cost for houses less than $300,000—thus, a $200,000 house will normally take seven months to complete. Ninety percent of the work may be done in less time, but the final details have a way of dragging on; if you want to plan ahead, this makes a good rule of thumb. On every job days will be lost for one reason or another, and these must be taken into account when estimating the completion date.

A typical schedule for a $180,000 wood frame house might run something like the following example:

Step	*Number of Weeks*
1. Clearing and final siting	1
2. Excavation and footing preparation	1—1½
3. Foundations	2—2½
4. Ground-floor framing and subfloor	1
5. Damp-proofing, drain tiles, and backfill	1
	6—7
6. Framing and partial sheathing (topping-off party, usually 8 to 9 weeks after starting)	2
7. Finish sheathing, fascias, soffits (start chimney)	1
8. Roofing and flashing work	1
9. Set windows and exterior doors and miscellaneous details (roughing of electrical, H.V.A.C., plumbing)	2
10. Siding	2—3
	8—9

Basic shell completed in about 3½ months

Step	Number of Weeks
11. Insulation, stairs, miscellaneous framing	1
12. Wallboard and spackling	1½—2
13. Interior trim, doors, hardware	2—3
14. Underlayment and flooring	1—1½
15. Cabinets installed, miscellaneous details	1—1½
16. Bookcases, built-ins, tile work	1½—2
17. Painting	2—2½
18. Set fixtures, electrical plates	1
19. Clean up and punch list; certificate of occupancy	1—1½
	12—16
	26—32 *

Moving Day

*6 months (26 weeks) @ $30,000 = $180,000
7½ months (32 weeks) @ $24,000 = $180,000

THE AUTHOR'S HOUSE, 1975. "*Upon the raising of the ridge pole of every proper house, ancient custom decrees the 'planting' of a branch of evergreen at the highest peak. Ceremonially set 'twixt earth and sky we celebrate the golden bough . . . its verdant color bright through darkest winter and its cones rich with the seeds of promise. So we foregather, invoking the spirit of the sacred tree, to partake the feast, lending to us and our guests the hint of the shelter to come, the stout walls, rafters and roof—the warmth of its hearth stones and forever more fecundity and joy to every dweller here.*"

—*John P. T. Blake*

Topping-Off Party

The framing, which is completed about 8 to 9 weeks after starting, seems to proceed so quickly that it is hard to imagine why a house takes so long to build. After months of planning, the sight of a framed house is a most gratifying experience. Everyone involved feels elated, and it is a tradition from ancient times to celebrate the completion of the framing with a ceremonial rite.

In our Western culture, the evergreen tree with its coniferous fruit has symbolized a permanence and stability independent of time and seasons, with the cones representing the bounteous fecundity of nature. Tree cults persisted for thousands of years (and are still evident at Christmastime). The custom of placing an evergreen bough on the ridgepole of a newly framed house was brought to America by the earliest European colonists—long before they brought the custom of the Christmas tree. (The Christmas tree, in fact, was not commonplace until the 1860s except in German communities.)

A Minoan signet ring dating from 2000 B.C. shows an evergreen tree on the pediment of a temple shrine. Perhaps originally intended to propitiate the anthropomorphic tree deity and induce him to favor the new house with children and other blessings, it has become an established and ubiquitous tradition. The occasion is celebrated by a party for all involved, with the owners providing the food and drink. This rite is so entrenched in the building tradition that I have even seen boughs topping off the steel skeletons of New York City skyscrapers.

Who Does What When

It is not within the scope of this book to describe each and every step in the building process, but it is appropriate to point out certain specific procedures and who is responsible for what.

The Contractor

Until the house is completed and the final payment made to the contractor, he considers it "his" house, and his workmen develop a proprietary interest in the project. The contractor organizes his jobs according to his own particular procedures and generates the momentum of the process. If he is a good leader, the subcontractors respond to his decisive enthusiasm and perform well. It is important that both you

Typical form of proposal (sometimes called "bid form").

FORM OF PROPOSAL   Date: *Jan 15ᵀᴴ, 1987*

FROM: *A. B.C. Construction Company, Sometown, N.Y.*

TO: *Mr & Mrs H.R. Smith,*

c/o JOHN MILNES BAKER A.I.A., Architect
Girdle Ridge Road, Katonah, New York 10536

RE: *A House for*   Arch't. Job # *400*
     Mr & Mrs H.R. Smith, Sometown, N.Y.

In compliance with your request for an "Upset Price", the
undersigned offers to provide all labor, materials, equipment
and contractor's services and to perform all operations necess..y
to complete the project in complete conformity with the Drawings
and Specifications prepared by architect John Milnes Baker A.I.A.
and dated: *Dec 1ˢᵀ, 1986* , for a sum ....

NOT TO EXCEED .... $ *200,000*

This price includes a Contractor's Fee of $ *18,000*

Any savings approved by the architect shall be divided equally
between the owner and the contractor.

All work shall be performed in a workmanlike manner and in
accordance with the requirements of the "General Conditions of
the Contract for Construction" (A.I.A. Document A201).

We can complete the work in approximately *Two Hundred* (*200*)
calendar days from receipt of the authorization to proceed.

This offer expires in thirty days.

BY: *Alexander B. Carlton* Date: *Jan 15, 1987*
                    President
     ABC Construction Company, Inc.

and the architect encourage this momentum by trying not to interfere or become involved until the rhythm of the work is firmly established.

It is the contractor's function to build the house as accurately and as well as he can. It behooves him to confer with the architect as much as is necessary to be absolutely sure that every aspect of the job is clear in his own mind.

The contractor is responsible for supervising the work of all the trades and is required to guarantee that all work is done in strict accordance with the construction documents. Even if the architect fails to notice a variation or misinterpretation that the contractor has made, that does not relieve the contractor of the responsibility to correct the work later on. In fact, the builder is liable for defects in his work up to the time laid down by the statute of limitations. His close scrutiny of the drawings and consultation with the architect are, therefore, in his own best interests.

At the end of each month the contractor prepares his "requisition for payment" and submits it to the architect for approval. This usually consists of a bill or statement showing the original sum allowed for each category of work, the amount expended to date, and the amount expended in the last month. Thus you and the architect can see at a glance how well they are keeping within the budget. (See pages 124-26.)

From the second requisition on, it is an excellent policy to have the contractor accompany his requisition with an affidavit stating that all previously requisitioned monies which were received on account for the indicated trades were indeed paid to those subcontractors and vendors. This procedure assures both you and the architect that there can be no liens filed by a supplier or subcontractor. In residential work, this policy is often deferred until the last couple of payments.

Establishing this practice from the beginning is a sound precaution, however, and no contractor should object, particularly if the architect supplies him with sufficient copies of the forms which he simply dates, signs, and notarizes each month. The notarization of the signature is mandatory to make the affidavit a valid legal document.

The Architect

During the construction phase of the work, the architect "administers" the contract. He is your agent, but he is also an impartial arbiter between you and the contractor.

First page of monthly requisition showing summary of account.

REQUISITION No. **4**   Date: July 7 '87   Period from June 1st to June 30th

PROJECT: *H.R. SMITH HOUSE*   Architect's Job No. **400**

ARCHITECT: JOHN MILNES BAKER A.I.A., Girdle Ridge Road, Katonah, New York 10536

CONTRACTOR: *ABC CONSTRUCTION, SOMETOWN, N.Y.*

Application is hereby made for payment on the subject project for work completed in accordance with the contract. The status of the account is shown on page 2 of this requisition.

ORIGINAL CONTRACT SUM .... $ *200,000.00*

Net changes by change order (# *1*   ) .... $ *1,250.00*

CONTRACT SUM TO DATE .... $ *201,250.00*

TOTAL COMPLETED AND STORED TO DATE .... $ *108,007.60*

Plus portion of Contractor's $ *18,000* fee .... $ *5,000.00*

TOTAL EARNED TO DATE .... $ *113,007.60*

LESS PREVIOUS CERTIFICATES FOR PAYMENT .... $ *89,500.00*

AMOUNT OF THIS REQUISITION .... $ *23,507.60*

AFFIDAVIT:

State of *NEW YORK*   County of *WESTCHESTER*

The undersigned contractor certifies that the work covered by this requisition has been completed in accordance with the contract documents and that he has paid all vendors and subcontractors and has satisfied all indebtedness incurred by him in conjunction with this project with the monies he has been paid by the owner in accordance with the architect's previous Certificates for Payment.

CONTRACTOR: *A.B.C CONSTRUCTION COMPANY INC.*

By: *Alexander B. Carlton*   Date: *July 7, 1987*

Subscribed and sworn to me this *7th* day of *July*   , 1987

NOTARY PUBLIC: *Barclay Morrison*   whose commmission expires *Aug 10 '89*

CERTIFICATE FOR PAYMENT:

In accordance with the contract and this application for payment, the contractor is entitled to payment in the amount of this requisition.

APPROVED FOR PAYMENT   By *John Milnes Baker*   Date: *7/8/87*

NOTE: This certificate is not negotiable. It is payable only to the payee named herein and its issuance, payment and acceptance are without prejudice to the rights of the owner or contractor under their agreement.

Page two shows current status of account.

REQUISITION No. **4**   Date: √ᴜʟʏ 7ᵗʰ   Period from √ᴜɴᴇ 1ˢᵀ to √ᴜɴᴇ 30ᵗʰ

PROJECT: _H.R. SMITH HOUSE_   Architect's Job No. **400**

ARCHITECT: JOHN MILNES BAKER A.I.A., Girdle Ridge Road, Katonah, N.Y. 10536

CONTRACTOR: _A.B.C. CONSTRUCTION COMPANY ᴵᴺᶜ_

SCHEDULE OF VALUES:

COST CATEGORY	CURRENT VALUE	PREVIOUS COST	+	CURRENT COST	=	TOTAL TO DATE	BALANCE TO COMPLETE
LUMP SUM							
Basic Shell	55,000	50,000.	+	5,000.	=	55,000.	—.
Overhead	7,000	3,000.	+	1,000.	=	4,000.	3,000.
Ext. Stain	1,500	1,500.	+	—.	=	1,500.	—.
Insulation	2,500	2,500.	+	—.	=	2,500.	—.
Drywall/spklg	9,500	2,500.	+	2,500.	=	5,000.	4,500.
Int. Doors Trim	9,000	—.	+	—.	=	—.	9,000.
H.V.A.C.	12,500	6,000.	+	2,000.	=	8,000.	4,500.
Plumbing	11,500	4,000.	+	1,500.	=	5,500.	6,000.
Electric	8,000	3,000.	+	1,500.	=	4,500.	3,500.
Total	116,500	72,500.	+	13,500.	=	86,000.	30,500.
ALLOWANCES							
Sitework	3,500	1,500.	+	—.	=	1,500.	2,000.
Fireplace/chm.	7,500	1,500.	+	3,000.	=	4,500.	3,000.
Windows/Ext doors	10,000	9,000.	+	257.60	=	9,257.60	*SAVED [742.40]
Flooring	6,000	—.	+	—.	=	—.	6,000.
Tile work	1,500	—.	+	—.	=	—.	1,500.
Cabinets	8,000	—.	+	2,500.	=	2,500.	5,500.
Decks & rails	6,000	—.	+	—.	=	—.	6,000.
Painting	6,000	—.	+	—.	=	—.	6,000.
Well & pump	3,500	—.	+	3,000.	=	3,000.	500.
Sewage Disp.	3,500	—.	+	—.	=	—.	3,500.
Miscellaneous	10,000	—.	+	—.	=	—.	10,000.
Total	65,500	12,000.	+	8,757.60	=	20,757.60	44,742.40
BLDRS. FEE	18,000	3,750.	+	1,250.	=	5,000.	13,000.
CONTRACT	# 200,000	88,250.	+	23,507.60	=	111,757.60	88,242.40
Change Orders ...	1,250	1,250.	+	—.	=	1,250.	—.
ADJUSTED CONTRACT	#201,250	89,500.	+	23,507.60	=	113,007.60	88,242.40

* #742.40 SAVING WILL BE ADDED TO THE #10,000 MISCELLANEOUS IN REQ #5

NOTE: Reimbursable expenses or "anticipated extras" as noted shall be paid
    with a separate check.

Third page of requisition is the actual invoice.

REQUISITION No. 4 Date: July 1 '87 Period from June 1 '87 to June 30, '87

FROM: A BC CONSTRUCTION COMPANY   CONTRACTOR
          SOMETOWN , NEW YORK

TO: MR & MRS H.R. SMITH , SOMETOWN , N.Y   OWNER
        c/o John Milnes Baker A.I.A., Girdle Ridge Road, Katonah, New York 10536

RE: A HOUSE FOR
        MR & MRS H.R. SMITH , SOMETOWN , N.Y.

The following work has been completed in accordance with the contract documents
and payment is now due:

DESCRIPTION OF WORK	Approx.	% completed	AMOUNT DUE

CURRENT COSTS (Costs incurred during this period)

		AMOUNT
LUMP SUM	OVERHEAD	$ 1,000.00
	BASIC SHELL (BAL. OF ROOF'G)	5,000.00
	DRYWALL (ON ACCOUNT)	2,500.00
	H.V.A.C. "	2,000.00
	PLUMBING "	1,500.00
	ELECTRICAL "	1,500.00
	TOTAL	$ 13,500.00
ALLOWANCES	FIREPLACES	3,000.00
	EXTERIOR DOORS & WINDOWS (BAL)	257.60
	CABINETS	2,500.00
	WELL	3,000.00
	TOTAL	$ 8,757.60
FEE		$ 1,250.00

TOTAL AMOUNT OF THIS BILL.......... Check # 1 for ....$ 23,507.60

PLEASE PAY THE FOLLOWING BILL WITH A SEPARATE CHECK:

REIMBURSABLE EXPENSES:

The following expenses were incurred during this period for "anticipated
extras" and are separate from the contract sum. These items are described in
the Supplementary General Conditions as "N.I.C." (Not-in-contract).

DESCRIPTION OF EXPENSE:	AMOUNT DUE
BAL OF SURVEYOR'S BILL	$ 550.00

TOTAL AMOUNT OF THIS BILL.......... CHECK # 2 for .... $ 550.00

The architect makes periodic site visits, observes the work, issues instructions to the builder, and helps the builder interpret the drawings, but unless he is also serving as construction manager, he does not *supervise* the work. He cannot be on the job every day, sitting on a sawhorse and overseeing every detail of the work—that is the contractor's job. The architect is responsible for clarifying each detail as it arises, and as the job progresses he issues supplementary drawings known as instruction sheets. These documents clarify the work expected under the contract.

If the contractor feels that the work described in an instruction sheet is outside the scope of the contract or in excess of an agreed allowance, he will request an "extra." If the architect acknowledges the validity of the claim, he can prepare a "change order" describing the extra work and indicating the amount requested. The owner must sign the change order before the work is performed. Otherwise the work must be redesigned with respect to the original budget or allowance.

No matter how carefully an architect has prepared the drawings and specifications, and no matter how carefully you have reviewed them, little incidental and unexpected extras always arise. Your assurance that "it can't cost much—go ahead," can create a real problem. A change order processed for each and every whim you may have—a pegboard behind the utility room door, extra shelves for storage in the cellar, installing a plastic door for the dog's house—can add up very quickly to an alarming amount. I always feel that an owner should allow a substantial sum, separate from any contingency figure, for just such minor items.

The contractor can be instructed to keep a running account of such incidentals to be incorporated into one change order whenever the accumulated sum equals $300 (or some other mutually agreeable amount). It is normally not advisable to leave an accumulated list of extras until the end of the job.

Often it is better to avoid breaking the contractor's momentum by not ordering such minor changes as garbage-can enclosures, workbenches, and shelving in the garage until the main job is completed and then having them done by a local carpenter-handyman. Most communities have such a craftsman who often does excellent work and will charge substantially less than the contractor because he has no overhead costs.

In addition to the "certificate for payment" or "recommendation for payment" forms, which the architect forwards to you once he has reviewed the contractor's requisition, the architect reviews "shop drawings" and "samples" which are submitted to him for approval before various component parts of the house are constructed or equipment is installed.

Shop drawings, prepared by suppliers or manufacturers for items such as stairs, cabinet work, metal work, and any special millwork, are submitted to the contractor in triplicate. He checks them first for general conformity. Unless there is some glaring deficiency, they are forwarded to the architect for his review. The architect either approves them, disapproves them, or stamps them "Approved as Noted," that is, approved subject to any specific changes noted by the architect. No work calling for approved shop drawings in the specifications can be started prior to the receipt of the architect's written approval, and the contractor is liable for any work that is installed without the architect's go ahead.

The specifications call for the submission of samples of floor coverings, stains, paints, brick, and so forth. The same ritual of approval as was needed for shop drawings is required for samples and for the catalog "cuts," copies of pages ripped from catalogs, of such items as heating and cooling equipment, electrical panel boxes, window units—virtually everything that was selected from a catalog.

The architect will approve some minor items without consulting you; but he will submit many others, such as plumbing fixtures, color samples, and wall finishes, for your final approval before returning them to the contractor.

There is a tendency to be casual and informal with respect to this procedure. The process can seem superfluous, but many errors are caught this way by providing an opportunity for last-minute reconsideration.

Additional services are sometimes performed by the architect before a building project is complete. These are discussed in the appendix ("The Architect's Fee") but three services that are not normally covered by his fee are noted here. They are:

1. Interior design and other services required for the selection of furnishings.
2. Preparation of reproducible record drawings—"as built" drawings—showing any significant changes in the work made during construction. (This is particularly true of alterations.)

3. Consultation concerning replacement of any work which has been damaged by fire or any services required because of major defects in the work of the contractor in the performance of the construction contract.

The Owner

Sometimes you as the owner may feel left out during the construction period. The architect spends more time talking to the builder than to you, and all that you seem to be expected to do is to approve samples and pay the bills. Most of the attention that the architect paid you during the design and working drawings phases is cut off. Many clients feel a need to keep as closely in touch with the architect as ever but, in fact, it is not necessary for the successful execution of the work at the early stages of construction.

Naturally you will have questions; keep a notebook and periodically arrange a meeting with the architect and review them all at the same time. Do not, except under the most extraordinary circumstances, call the builder at his home in the evening with questions that can be answered by the architect.

Here are a few ground rules that it is advisable to follow:

DO NOT   give directions to the builder, except of the most minor kind, and never to his subcontractors or workmen.

DO NOT   approve work that the builder has done. In some instances an owner who has okayed a job may have to assume responsibility for work that has not been correctly executed. By the same token, do not reject work; that is your architect's role. Take up any complaints with him.

DO NOT   argue with your architect in front of the builder. Anything which undermines the architect's role will only backfire on you.

DO NOT   make design decisions with the builder, or allow substitutions without written change orders prepared by the architect.

DO NOT   hold up progress by delaying decisions with respect to flooring, tiles, colors, finishes.

DO   visit the job as often as you like, but do not interrupt the progress of the work. Make all the complimentary comments you like, and ask questions of the foreman or builder, but don't expect lengthy explanations—they have their work to do.

DO   bring an occasional container of coffee on a chilly day, or a six-pack of beer if you happen to visit in the late afternoon. A courteous and respectful owner who appreciates the efforts of the workmen goes a long way toward making a happy and productive team.

DO   try to visit the site with your architect from time to time, occasionally without the builder. You will be freer to air complaints, ask questions, and review decisions that do not directly affect the builder and need not occupy his time.

DO   *pay bills promptly,* and always pay the precise amount indicated by the architect. Rounding off amounts confuses everyone's bookkeeping. The architect usually receives the contractor's requisition for payment about the third day of the month. He approves it by the fifth or sixth with the issuance of his "recommendation for payment and statement of account," and it is payable by the tenth day of each month.

Completion

Near the end of the job the builder will announce that he is finished and wants to submit his final requisition. The architect makes a thorough inspection of the house, often with both the owner and the builder, and makes notes of any deficiencies of even the most minor sort. These notes constitute the "punch list," and all the items listed must be remedied before the job is completed. Naturally, only items specifically within the contract are on this list. You may have an assortment of afterthoughts and extras—garbage-can enclosures, a workbench, or extra cupboards; unless these are left for a handyman to do later, they must be listed separately and covered by either a change order or a separate arrangement between you and the builder. Since this is totally outside the contract, it should not determine when the builder gets paid for the work described in the contract documents.

In addition to completion of the work described in the punch list, the contractor must submit *to the architect*, for his review, the "Certificate of Occupancy" issued by the local building department and required before the premises can be legally occupied. The certificate of occupancy is accompanied by "Release of Lien" forms from all vendors and subcontractors, or a final notarized affidavit from the contractor, and by all warranties for the mechanical equipment installed by the contractor.

At this point the builder has fulfilled his obligations under the A.I.A. contract. The architect reviews the material and completes the recommendation for payment form. You then write your last check to the contractor. This payment is normally due within ten days of the architect's approval.

Arbitration

The standard A.I.A. contracts include what is called an arbitration clause. This is an agreement between the owner and the contractor or the owner and architect (it forms part of both contracts) to settle any "claims, disputes or other matters in question" in accordance with the Construction Industry Arbitration Rules of the American Arbitration Association.

Basically, the partners to the contract agree to accept the judgment of an arbiter in the event of any dispute. The arbitration process is simpler, less costly, and less time-consuming than litigation and is generally far more efficient and satisfactory.

One possible drawback is that because the arbiter's judgment is final, there is no recourse open to the losing party. The members of the arbitration panel are invariably experienced professionals (lawyers, architects, engineers) and the judgments are generally accepted as being fair and equitable.

. . . hundreds of insignificant, unpleasing or down-right ugly houses can be turned into dwellings of charm—if their proportions are within reason—sometimes even when they are not.

Emily Post
The Personality of a House

4 REMODELING
Alterations and Additions

There are basically four kinds of remodeling: renovation, restoration, alteration, and addition. Renovation is limited to renewal of existing surfaces and is really glorified maintenance work. Though an architect can be helpful on the more complex jobs, and can usually be retained at an hourly rate to consult with the owner, on a simpler job where what needs to be done is clear, a competent builder is all that is needed.

Restoration work is more apt to be architectural; that is, the aim is literally to put back an old building into its original condition. The purpose of restoration work, in the strictest sense, is to refurbish a building without any modernization—generally undertaken not by the home-owner but by museums. As soon as heat is added to an eighteenth-century farmhouse or modern conveniences are incorporated into an old building, we are in the realm of alterations.

PRELIMINARY CONSIDERATIONS

Before you plunge into an expensive project, it is prudent to consider what you want to accomplish by remodeling. Economics certainly plays a role and the investment aspect is worth considering. The big question is how much you should spend.

If you are remodeling because you want to sell your house in six months, you should expect a high return on your investment. An expenditure of $10,000 that increases the value of your house by $25,000 is obviously money well spent. This, however, is not the most typical reason for remodeling a house.

At the other end of the spectrum you have an owner who wants to put $200,000 into his house for a swimming pool and an addition. He realizes that in doing so he will then own the most expensive house on the block. His chances of selling the house for $200,000 more than its value before remodeling are slim. Yet everyone in his family loves their home, they all have strong ties to the community, and they don't really want to move. What he does want is a pool and more space. Remodeling may not be the best financial investment in the world, but he is doing it for good, sound reasons.

Probably 75 percent of the people who remodel fall between these two extremes. Most often the person contemplating a remodeling project wants to make his house more livable, but he wants the cost of the project to be reflected in the increased resale value of his house. A realistic budget must be established—an appropriate amount of money to put into the remodeling project that you can count on recouping if and when you sell.

I was recently asked to look at an old house a couple had just bought at an inflated price of $500,000. There were so many things wrong with it that they could easily have spent another $200,000 on the house and still not have their swimming pool. Even then there would have been inherent faults that simply could not have been rectified. I could not see how they would ever get their $700,000 back, let alone make a profit.

I strongly urged them to resell the house, find some land, and build a new house with their $700,000. The new house would not only suit their needs infinitely better than anything that could have been done to their old house, but the new one would probably have a resale value of over one million dollars. The $300,000 bonus equity is not to be taken lightly!

In another instance I urged a couple to consider demolishing their house and starting from scratch on their own property. The house was small and nondescript and in terrible shape but on land that had appreciated over the years that they had lived there to well over $200,000. It made no sense at all to remodel a junky house that was very badly sited on the property. They already owned the land and could also continue to live in their present house while the new one was under construction. The new house might cost fifty to a hundred thousand more than the remodeling of the old one, but when the project was finished the equity they would have in the new house would be easily worth two or three times that amount.

These instances may be unusual, but in considering all the aspects of remodeling I think it behooves one to consider even rather drastic alternatives. In any event, if you do decide to simply redo the kitchen and add on a sun space you will have the satisfaction of knowing you examined all the possibilities open to you.

ALTERATIONS AND ADDITIONS

The entire process outlined in the previous chapters is pertinent to alteration work, whether it is limited to an existing building or includes an enlargement of the structure by an addition. In a sense, the process of altering a house is exactly like any other house-building project, except that the program (both functional and architectural) is partly predetermined. The parameters within which the architect works are narrowed considerably, but the same process of analysis, programming, and design study occurs as used in building a new house. Alteration work has a few added complications, however.

Measured Drawings

The first step in any alteration work is to obtain an accurate set of drawings of the existing building. If the original drawings are not available, measured drawings must be made. This should be done even when contemplating such apparently minor additions as, for instance, a screened porch. To the trained eye of the architect a set of measured drawings will often disclose unforeseen difficulties, such as a poor circulation pattern, or unexpected solutions which would not have occurred to the owner. Even if the original drawings do exist, they may not be "as-built" drawings and should be checked for their accuracy. Modifications are often made during the construction phase of a house, and the original working drawings may not have been changed accordingly.

An architect can usually measure a house in a few hours, and he can record the key dimensions on a ⅛-inch-scale "sketch plan" in a day. Precisely drawn "as-built" drawings may not be required for the schematic design stage of an alteration project, so the architect's fee is not apt to be more than three or four hundred dollars, and might even be considerably less.

Whether an architect or the owner does the measured drawings, certain conventions should be followed so the drawings can be interpreted by anyone referring to them. The following illustration outlines the process and should be helpful to any owner choosing to make his or her own set.

How to Measure a House

Get yourself a clipboard and a couple of sharp pencils, a 6-foot folding rule (preferably one with an extension on one end), a 50-foot metal tape (one with feet and inches), a 6-inch architect's scale (or some ⅛-inch graph paper), and some paper. Try to find someone to hold the "dumb" end of the tape. (When my children were only three years old, they could manage this job!)

First measure the entire perimeter—the masonry foundation—and draw it to ⅛-inch scale. Then hold the end of the tape at each corner and measure the openings in each wall. Measure the actual size of the window sashes and doors. You can reduce the margin of error by extending the 50-foot tape the full length of the wall and reading off the distance from the corner. (Be sure to hold the end of the tape slightly in from the edge of the building so that it lines up with the corner of the foundation.)

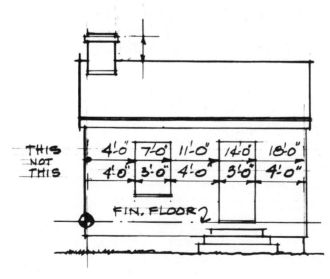

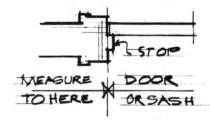

The window and door measurements should be made to the window sash (the part that moves) and to the actual door itself.

After recording the distance from the finished floor to the bottom of the siding, check the distance from the bottom of the siding to the finish grade at each corner of the house. The vertical dimensions of the windows and doors are more easily measured on the inside.

Measure all the interior spaces—finish wall to finish wall (not the baseboards)—and record all pertinent data. Be sure to indicate the thickness of each wall, which can easily be measured at the door jambs: show the height of the ceiling and the distance from finish floor to finish floor in a two-story house. This can best be measured at the stairwell.

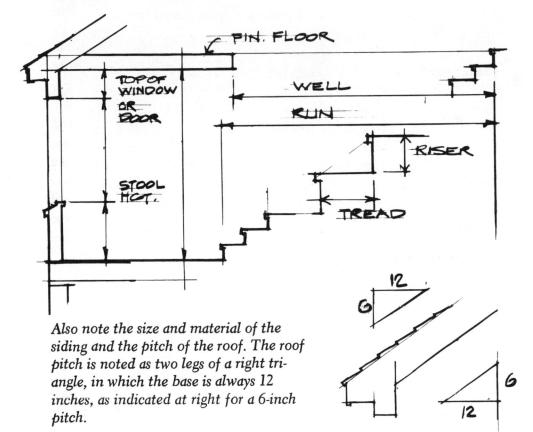

Also note the size and material of the siding and the pitch of the roof. The roof pitch is noted as two legs of a right triangle, in which the base is always 12 inches, as indicated at right for a 6-inch pitch.

Careful note should be made of any unusual structural and mechanical features that would be difficult to change, such as steel beams, major electrical conduits, masonry, duct shafts, and radiators. Photographs (inside and out) are extremely helpful and should always be made with a 6-foot rule placed against the wall for scale.

Once the measured drawings (including a site plan showing trees, driveway, and garden areas) are made, the process of programming and design can begin precisely as outlined in the earlier chapters.

Master Plan

I must emphasize that before making *any* changes in an old house—even before painting—it is worthwhile to measure the house, make up a set of ⅛-inch-scale plans, and review them with an architect. These plans can even be helpful to movers, as you can indicate where you want boxes placed when they are removed from the van.

I can think of several instances when I was called in for advice a year or so after a couple had bought a house. In one case a glance at the floor plans revealed a blatantly obvious defect in the circulation pattern which could have been remedied easily and inexpensively before they moved into the house by relocating a doorway. But the new house owners, reluctant to engage an architect for even an initial review, had hired the local handyman to build urgently needed bookcases right where the door opening should have been, and to put up a special (now out of print) wallpaper on another partition. The cost of the bookcases and the expense of redoing the room made the owners reluctant to change these new "improvements" and swallow the double cost.

Whatever changes are contemplated, no matter how trivial, it is worth studying the entire picture and outlining various options, each of which can be effected independently, while contributing to a unified plan that maximizes the potential amenities of the house.

Clients who are thinking of remodeling are often deterred by two common misunderstandings. One is the assumption that, in order to find the space they need, they must have an addition. Frequently, the existing square footage is adequate but underutilized. An architect can often find space within the existing shell that answers the programmed requirements.

A second fallacy is that moving walls and partitions is terribly expensive. This is simply not the case, particularly if the house is of wood frame construction. Stud walls can be removed, replaced, and relocated with relative ease. The most dramatic results are often obtained for comparatively little money.

COKER STUDIO

This two-car garage came with Paul Coker, Jr.'s, property. It was converted to a studio and guest cottage and served as a dwelling while the main house was under construction.

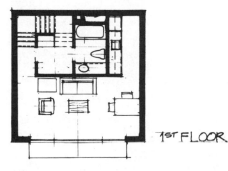

2ND FL

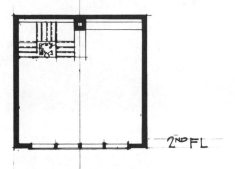

1ST FLOOR

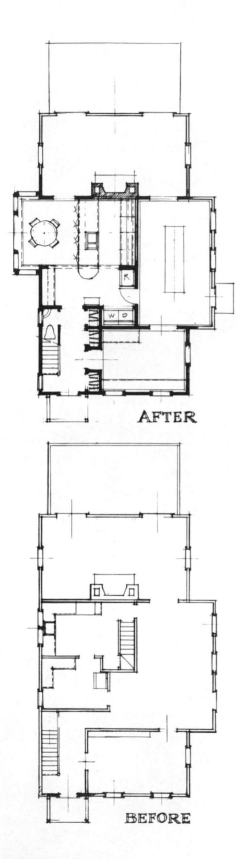

AFTER

BEFORE

View of the breakfast area, looking from the new opening between the kitchen and the living room.

View looking toward kitchen work space from the breakfast area.

KNOWLES KITCHEN
The original kitchen in this Connecticut farmhouse was dreary and constricted. After opening up walls and arranging a fluid circulation flow, the owners can now accommodate large groups at their numerous buffet dinners.

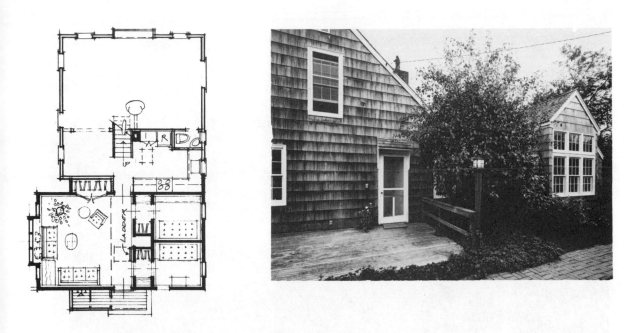

The addition to the Webbs' weekend house duplicates the character of the original building—on the outside.

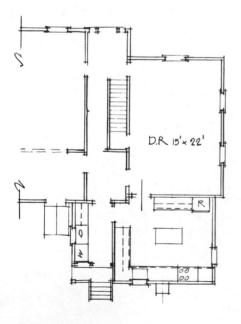

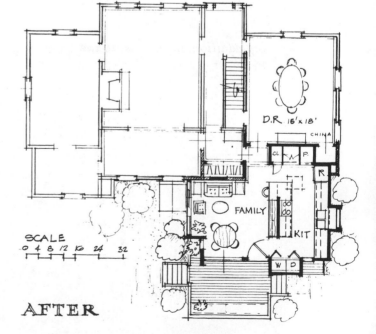

BEFORE

AFTER

BORG ADDITION

The Borg addition, in contrast to the Webb addition shown on page 141, makes no attempt to look like an original part of the house (opposite above), though its unassertive flat roof, its texture, and its modest scale complement the original nineteenth-century structure. The floor plans on the opposite page show how the addition utilized the old foundation of the demolished kitchen wing and "borrowed" some space from the excessively large dining room of the original house.

Above: *The kitchen storage wall divides the work area from the family room.*

Right: *Detail of the breakfast area.*

KERNAN ADDITION

The Kernans' original kitchen was isolated from the rest of the house and had no place to sit. The enlarged kitchen works better and opens to a new family room with informal dining and easy access to a new terrace.

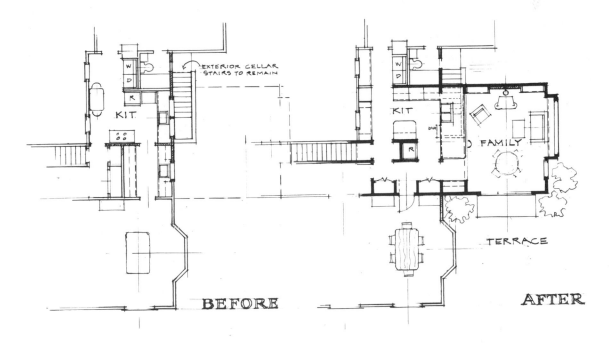

EXTERIOR CELLAR
STAIRS TO REMAIN

W
D
R

KIT.

BEFORE

W
D
R

KIT.

DW

FAMILY

TERRACE

AFTER

Above: *The Regan addition matches the original farmhouse.*

Below: *View of the new family room, looking toward the entry.*

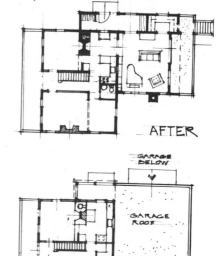

AFTER

BEFORE

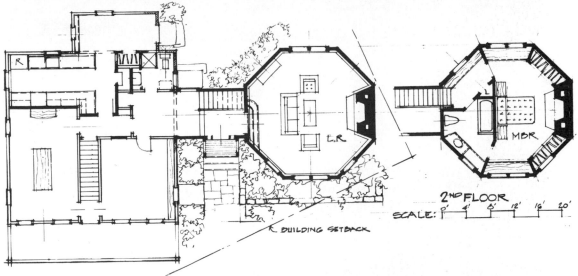

2ND FLOOR

SCALE: 0' 4' 6' 12' 16' 20'

L.R

MBR

R BUILDING SETBACK

ZIPSER ADDITION

The addition to this tiny early 1800s saltbox was restricted by setback limitations and by the steep rocky hillside at the rear. The octagon seemed to be the perfect solution.

The architect's goal is the enrichment of life through the use of structured form, disciplined space, and an ordered environment and nowhere can this be more fully achieved than in a family's dwelling.

J. M. B.

5 THE HARMONIOUS HOUSE
How to Judge the Merits of a House and Its Architect

There are certain basic principles on which any critical assessment of a house should be based. Even though your immediate response to any building is subjective and emotional, if you can analyze the reasons behind your spontaneous response, then not only will your understanding and enjoyment of architecture increase, but you will also be in a far better position to describe the kind of house you would like to your own architect.

The purpose of this chapter is to give you a set of standards with which you can evaluate your architect's ideas. The more knowledgeable you are, the more stimulating the challenge of designing your home will be to him.

I have already outlined the threefold process of building a house: the problem, the solution, and the implementation. Before you can make a valid critical evaluation of a house, each of these aspects must be thoroughly considered. This is particularly true of those contemporary houses that are not constructed following a set style or formula.

THE PROBLEM

The first question to consider in evaluating a house that has already been built is what problem the architect was trying to solve and what were the limits within which he had to work. The four principal constraints on design are the program, the physical features of the site, the local zoning and legal restrictions, and the budget.

The program, as you will remember, is the architect's attempt to create a house which will not only provide physical space for the family's various activities, but will also respond empathetically to each member's subjective needs. To evaluate the architect's interpretative talent effectively, you should do your best to determine what kind of people the owners are and how well the house suits their individual life-style.

Next in importance to the program come the limitations of the site. Consider the views, the vegetation, the prevailing wind, the drainage, topography, and climate. Has the architect used the site in such a way as to make the most of its good features and minimize its drawbacks?

In addition to the general climate of the locality, consider what is sometimes called the microclimate, or any peculiar climatic variations that affect different portions of the site. Two houses a hundred yards apart can have very different microclimates if one is on the north slope of a barren hill and the other on the southern side nestled in a grove of protective evergreens.

Virtually every community has some governmental agency which issues a permit to anyone erecting a house. Before it is issued, plans have to be submitted which show that the proposed house conforms to the requirements of the building codes with respect to minimum lot size, frontage (the amount of the lot which must border a road), and setbacks (the distances of any building, the sewage system, and the well, from the boundary lines of the lot). Wells and sewage systems must be a prescribed distance apart and require a considerable amount of open space—sometimes in an awkward position. In most enlightened communities wetlands are now controlled, and an architect is no longer free to build beside a brook or river. The question here should be: "How well did the architect handle the problem within the parameters established by law?"

Last but not least comes the budget. Money does not assure good design—in fact the reverse may be true—but a $75-per-square-foot house will naturally be much simpler than one with a $100-per-square-foot budget. A good architect thinks of ingenious ways of saving his clients money in the long run. Air conditioning, for instance, will be needed far less often if high clerestory windows in a central hall produce a circulatory effect which moves the air through the house by natural means. With a gentle movement of air, you may be perfectly comfortable at a temperature of 80 degrees Fahrenheit and only feel hot enough to switch on the air-conditioner when the temperature reaches 90 degrees.

Once you have an understanding of the problem which confronted the architect, you can then go on to judge the merits of the solution.

THE SOLUTION

Site Plan

In judging a house in terms of how effectively the architect solved the problem, it is important to consider the site plan. How effectively is the house positioned in relation to the road, the neighbors, the vistas, and the natural ambience? Is the house oriented to maximize the benefits from the sun and the prevailing breezes, and to minimize any drawbacks, such as poor drainage patterns, proximity of neighboring houses, and flat, sparsely planted property? Are the outdoor areas effectively planned in relation to the interior spaces? The driveway should be large enough to enable a car to turn around comfortably even when a couple of cars are parked. The garbage truck and the oil truck should have easy access, even in winter, and the garbage cans and service area should be unobtrusive, yet convenient. If there are young children, outdoor play areas should be visible from the kitchen window, yet they should be separate from the outdoor terrace or patio and the view from the living room.

In addition to the successful resolution of the many problems in placing a house on a given site, that elusive "extra something" should be evident—a sense of expectancy in entering a driveway, an inviting first glimpse of the front door, a planting which effectively complements the building, or a garden that contains a sequence of refreshing surprises. No site plan can be judged independently of the interior spaces; the site plan should be a logical and complementary extension of the floor plan of the house, and both must be judged together.

Floor Plan

The merits of the floor plan of a house depend not just on the size, proportion, and location of the various rooms, but also on how they are interconnected. It is, perhaps, the nonprogrammed spaces, such as the hallways and stairs, and the sequence of visual experiences they provide that infuse the floor plan with the life and richness of good architecture. Variety of light, space, and vista should result in a series of subtle surprises that contribute to the special quality of a house and contrast to the disciplined order of the floor plan.

The floor plan itself should offer a pleasing, ordered pattern with compatible spatial relationships. Furniture arrangements should be carefully worked out and the spaces must comfortably accommodate the furniture appropriate to each. There is no formula that will ensure a successful floor plan, but certain basic principles are universal and should be evident in any well-planned house. Circulation patterns should be direct and clear, the lines and planes crisp, and the basic pattern laid down in the parti developed to an integrated and logical conclusion.

Massing

The floor plan is essentially a study in planes, spatial only in the number of levels. The volumes defined by the structure and planes of the walls, floors, and roof are sculptural in their three-dimensionality. The shape or form of a house must, therefore, possess a sculptural integrity to produce the continuity and unity essential to any art.

As a form emerges from the floor plan, the interior spaces are expressed in the molded volumes of the whole. Emphasis is placed on the dominant spaces, the group-living rooms, with the smaller rooms subordinate in mass, as they are in plan. The mass and form must grow logically and inevitably from the plan.

There is a language of architecture, and a house should be as clear and articulate as an effective verbal expression. We expect to find a car, or at least the space for one, behind a garage door and a studio beneath a north skylight. If we are fooled, we feel cheated and contemptuously dismiss such an outrage, just as we would a pretentious and garbled literary effort, as incompetent.

Proportion

Proportion refers to the dimensional relationships of the components of an object or space and implies a relationship of those parts to the whole, as well as to each other. Several rooms in a house, for example, could have a height, width, and length ratio of 1:2:4 but be entirely different sizes; the 30-by-60-by-120-foot tennis court and the 8-by-16-by-32-foot family room have identical proportions, but because their functional requirements are different, they vary in size. These proportions, incidentally, are excellent for an enclosed tennis court (or a shoe box), but less appropriate for a living room.

The relationship of any component part of a building to the whole is in proportion if it is appropriate for its intended use and contributes to the cohesive unity of the overall design. A proportion of 7:5:7 means nothing by itself, but if it is expressed as 35:25:35, it may have a familiar ring to the followers of beauty contests. Change the first figure so that the proportion becomes 45:25:35, and the image becomes grotesque; the woman with the 45-inch bosom, no matter how shapely her legs or pretty her face, is no longer in the running for "Miss America." This analogy can be applied to architecture. For example, about the only thing a 1,200-square-foot bungalow with a four-car garage is appropriate for is a chauffeur's cottage on a large estate. The combination violates our sense of order and becomes an absurdity.

The success or failure of any design depends to a large extent on the sensitivity of the designer in establishing an appropriate ratio between the dimensions of an object or space and those of the form or volume of which it is a part. Whether one element of a whole has good proportions depends entirely upon the nature of the intended effect and whether it is suitable for the purpose for which it was designed, in both its physical functions and its aesthetic and emotional effect. In talking about proportions in architecture, we hardly ever discuss them in the abstract; we almost invariably imply a ratio of the size of the furniture to the room, the room to the house, the house to the lot, and all will be finally judged as they relate to the people they are designed for. Now we are talking about something even more abstract but just as real: scale.

Scale

Scale, like proportion, refers to the dimensional characteristics of various architectural elements, but the ratio relates to an objective, known standard—the human body. An object or space has human scale if its design is suitable to the human figure. Since the human body is the constant, countertop heights, steps, handrails, and benches are good elements to use to establish scale. A bank or an insurance company headquarters may have a monumental scale, with huge doorways and massive details designed to impress the customer with the importance of the institution, but the comfortable, easy scale of a residence is measured by a normal-sized person. Beds are a little over 6 feet, doorways 6 feet 8 inches high, windowsills 2 feet 6 inches, and countertops around 36 inches.

Variations in scale may be consciously designed to create a given effect. For example, a low-ceilinged entrance hall may lend greater impact to a living room of moderate size than a higher ceiling would; the smaller scale of a child's room may encourage him to play there rather than all over the house; and a modesty and refinement in the scale of its furniture may make a relatively small room seem gracious and inviting.

To the architect, then, scale is a means of expressing character and evoking an emotion in the viewer. In this sense scale becomes the architect's most vital tool in controlling the kind of response people will have to the environment he is creating. A sense of scale is intuitive, and we all respond to the subtlest changes. An architect may, by virtue of his training, be more aware of what means have been used to establish the scale of a particular room than the average layman, but he is no more sensitive to its effect.

In houses that become homes our sense of scale must be satisfied, our expectations fulfilled. Tables and chairs must be an appropriate size, doorways provide a comfortable space to pass through, and stairs accommodate our natural step. The overly quaint scale of "Ye Olde Inne" may appeal to the diner-out as an amusing contrast to his real life, but it would be a ridiculous affectation in a modern house, no more appropriate than a scaled-down version of Mount Vernon would look on a suburban street.

Man is the basic measure by which we assess the scale of an object, be it a room, a house, or a village street, and in a drawing or model the proportion between an arbitrarily assumed height for man and the object or space depicted remains the same.

Character and Expression

Volumes and spaces are implicit in the floor plan. They are given definition and reality by the structure and materials from which the building is made. It is the expression of the structural system and the nature of the component parts, details as well as spaces, which complete the architectural statement.

Two wood-frame houses may be of identical shape and size and have exactly the same openings for the windows and doors. But their character and expression—that is, the texture, the color, the ornamentation, and the inherent quality of the materials used—can make them as different as soda pop is from a fine wine.

It is in this area that the question of taste arises—certainly a controversial and relative term and not one I intend to dwell on in this book. However, there are three basic criteria of good taste that I believe are fundamental, and I offer them for consideration. They are simplicity, honesty, and propriety.

Simplicity

Simplicity in the architectural sense implies a harmonious integration of all the component parts so that nothing is redundant no matter how intricate the details. An empty room or a stark, plain, unadorned building is not necessarily simple, but an Oriental rug is if the complexities of its pattern coordinate in a unified design. Ornament, if it is an integral part of the architecture and not applied decoration, does not detract from the simplicity of a building. In fact, if a building or any part of that building can be understood more easily by the enrichment and embellishment of certain elements, the textures and patterns actually contribute to the building's simplicity.

Honesty

The structural system of a building need not be glorified by exposure and emphasis, nor do the functions of every element have to be individually expressed. But whatever character and expression are evident in a building should somehow be derived from the nature of the building itself.

The functions of the spaces and volumes should be identifiable by the way they are expressed. A large skylight or window on the north side of a house says "studio"; the chimney mass at the heart of the largest element says "living room"; doors of various sizes and shapes say "Front door—Welcome," "garage door," "back door," and so on. As I said earlier, these constitute the basic language of architecture, and they should say what they mean.

There is almost no material that cannot be used effectively in a house, given imagination, ingenuity, and taste, but no material should ever be disguised to look like something else. Plastic laminate is a marvelous surface which comes in a wide range of colors and textures, but it becomes cheap imitation when used to simulate wood. Vinyl is an excellent material for floors, but why make it look like Spanish tile? Every material has its own nature, and any attempt to deny that nature usually results in an overall effect that is superficial and cheap, even if the cost is extremely high.

Propriety

Materials should be used in a way that is appropriate to their natures. Stone and concrete, for example, are inherently massive and capable of withstanding tremendous compressive forces. To use either as a "skin" or a veneer is to deny each its most characteristic quality.

I know of a ski lodge in Vermont that is built on wood-cased Lally columns, with a wood-cased steel beam carrying a rubble masonry wall above a filler panel of plate glass. These are totally inappropriate uses of the materials, and they are in bad taste. There is nothing inherently wrong with any of the materials; it is just the way they are put together.

Originality and Style

If a rational and logical plan is developed in three dimensions with simplicity, honesty, and propriety, and the mass or form has an appropriate proportion and scale, architecture *may* result. This is more likely if the design is executed with skill and proficiency and is unique to the particular project. However, there are no simple guarantees that the building will have its own inherent style rather than a derivative or reminiscent style associated with some other time and place. It will be "original" if the solution has evolved from the nature of the problem to be solved, even if the forms used are familiar and the materials traditional ones.

A quality house respects the nature of the terrain, and its materials appropriately complement the surroundings. This does not necessarily mean a home must mimic a geological formation; houses are man-made, and as such can stand separate from nature. A house on stilts can be as valid an approach to design as a berm house with a sod roof. But, whatever may have been a valid approach in the past, our awareness today of man's increasingly detrimental impact on the environment has dictated a far more sensitive and companionable relationship between man and nature, between the house and its site.

More and more houses are built in rural areas every year, and pockets of woodland and fields are forfeited forever. Consequently, a quiet and humble assertion of man's presence seems an appropriate attitude toward the development of any site.

If you use the criteria given in this chapter, you will still like or dislike a given house, but for sound objective and intellectual reasons, not because of a capricious and subjective whim.

The following portfolio of houses from the author's files will give you a chance to judge a variety of houses and to understand why they are so different one from the other, though each has an identifiable quality of the architect's predilections.

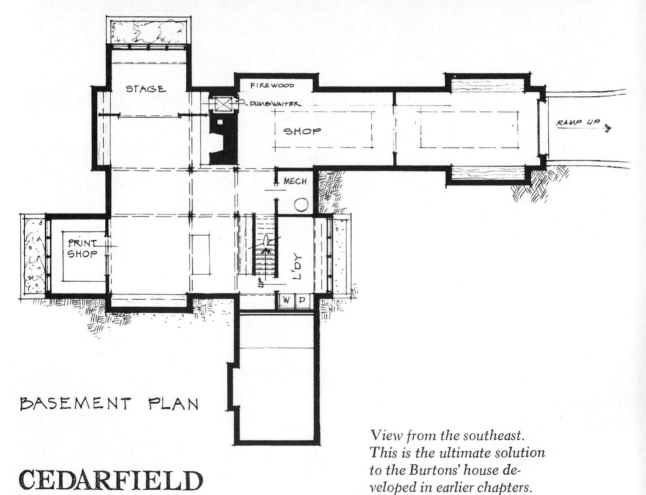

BASEMENT PLAN

CEDARFIELD

View from the southeast. This is the ultimate solution to the Burtons' house developed in earlier chapters.

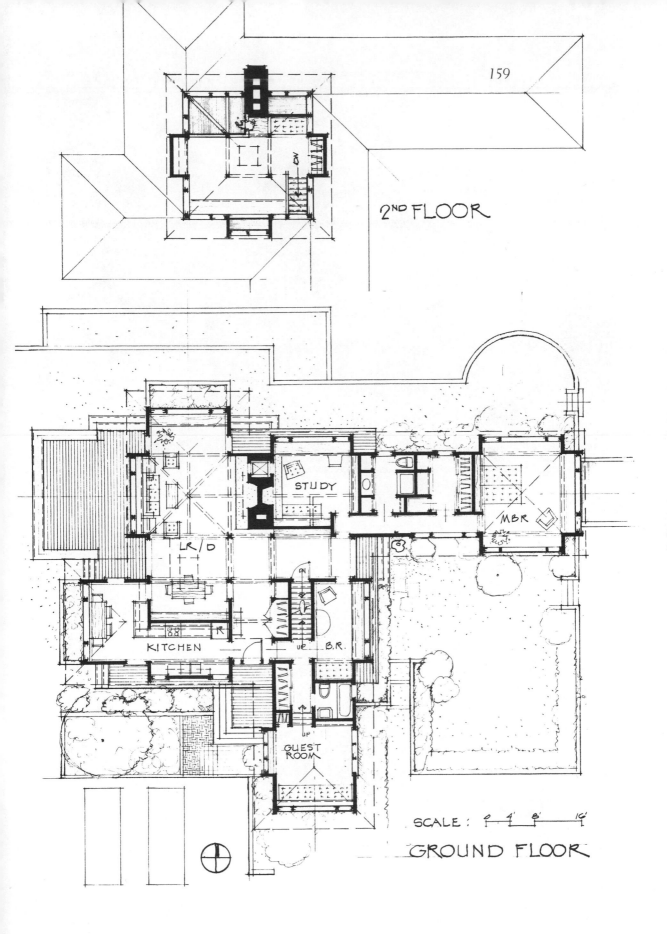

159

2ND FLOOR

STUDY

MBR

LR/D

KITCHEN

UP   B.R.

GUEST
ROOM

SCALE:

GROUND FLOOR

Exterior view of the deck as seen from the southwest.

Left: *The guest room.*

Opposite page: *The fireplace area of the living room, looking toward the entrance. Karen can be seen looking down from the "everything" room on the upper level.*

The client, a single person, owned an extraordinarily beautiful hilltop in Connecticut with a pond, an orchard, a stand of white pines, and an old stone wall near the crest of the hill. Vistas of distant ridges were possible from a second story, but it seemed a desecration to build on the very top of the site with its outcrops, cedar trees, and pampas grass. The house was therefore placed in a sloping meadow to the east of the stone wall (which ran north and south) and was connected to the hilltop by a bridge.

Two small tower rooms afford dramatic views of the surrounding countryside and serve as guest rooms and retreats. The living room and main guest room are at the entry level, with the guest bath serving as a powder room. The owner's bedroom and bath are located on the floor below, along with the kitchen and dining/sitting room with its own fireplace and easy access to the ample deck.

The lowest level contains the mechanical equipment, storage, and changing rooms for the pool. The area under the deck was planned as a lanai or screened porch next to the pool.

The owner wanted a warm house—"not too rustic"—that was not overly assertive on the site. With the owner's predilection for barns and silos, the idea of a tower was appealing.

BAEKELAND

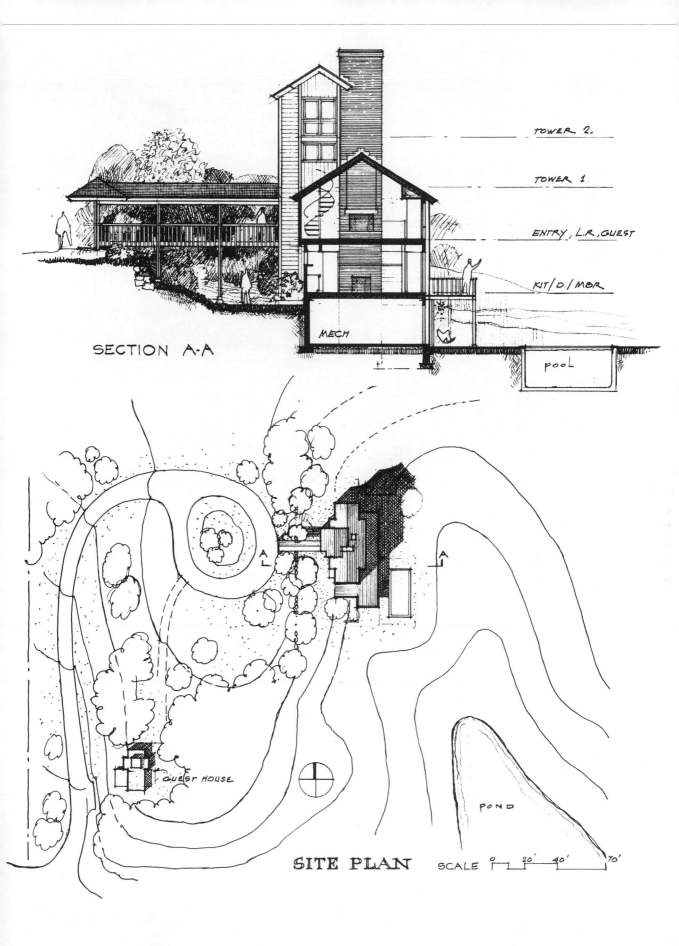

SECTION A·A

TOWER 2.

TOWER 1.

ENTRY, L.R., GUEST

KIT/D./MBR

MECH

POOL

GUEST HOUSE

POND

SITE PLAN SCALE 0 20' 40' 70'

View from the south.

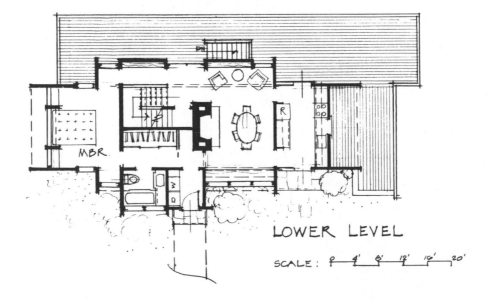

LOWER LEVEL

SCALE: 0   4'   8'   12'   16'   20'

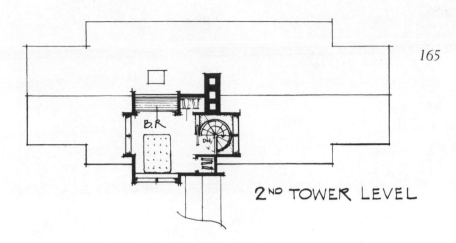

2ND TOWER LEVEL

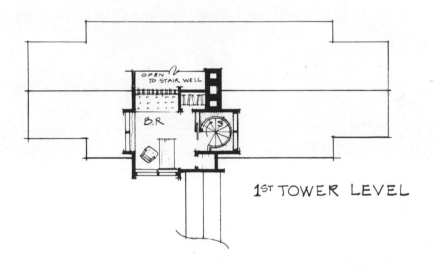

1ST TOWER LEVEL

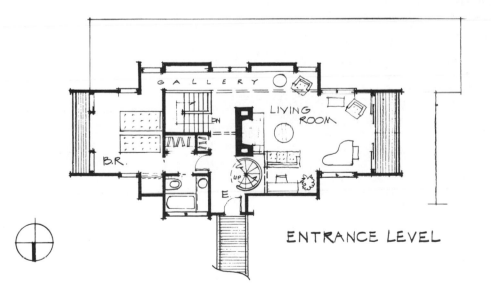

ENTRANCE LEVEL

165

Left: *The bridge leading to the main entrance, with the mudroom door below.*

Above: *The view of the front door from the bridge.*

Opposite page: *The upper view shows the living room from the entrance as seen through the circular stairway with the pond beyond. The visitor is drawn into the house and discovers the living room again around the massive brick fireplace wall.*

Above: *View from the driveway and guest parking.*

Below: *View from the northwest.*

Perhaps the most sculptured or geometric of all the houses in this book, it was designed for a creative couple with no children. Openness and inter-penetrating living spaces took precedence over the privacy required by larger families.

HERZOG

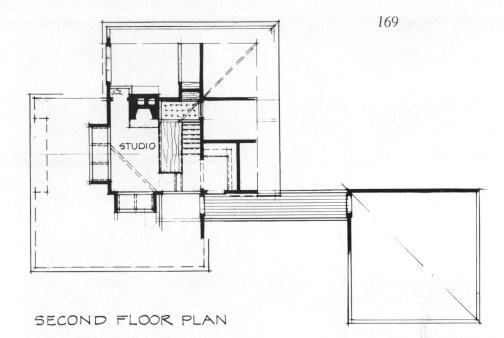

SECOND FLOOR PLAN

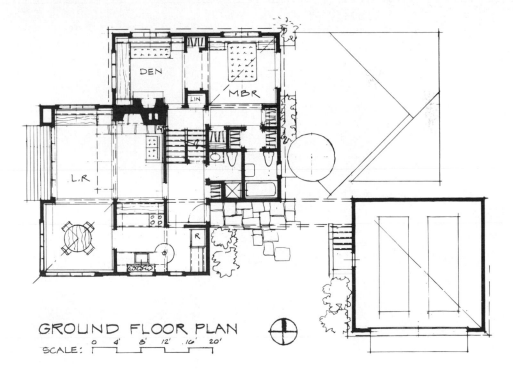

GROUND FLOOR PLAN

SCALE: 0 4'   8' 12' 16' 20'

Above: *View of the living room from the entryway. Note the fireplace on the right.*

Left: *Looking from the northwest corner of the living room toward the entryway and kitchen (see also page 44).*

Opposite (lower left): *Looking toward the master bedroom from the den.*

Opposite (lower right): *Studio seen from the head of the stairs.*

Opposite (top): *Studio, looking toward the fireplace and bunk above the stairway.*

Free-lance artist Paul Coker, who is a bachelor, purchased this brookside site, complete with driveway and a pre-World War II garage in sound condition—but no house.

The first project was to convert the garage into a studio/guest house for the owner to live in while his house was under construction.

The building site was low, but the views of the brook to the east, south, and west were unique and capivating. The view to the north toward the road was of no particular consequence.

The second-floor living room of the house, with its balcony and loft and the high-ceilinged master bedroom, give maximum expanse to the numerous vistas. The kitchen and dining room on the ground floor provide easy access to the ample deck, which overhangs the water.

The dominant chimney mass, which serves to anchor the house to the ground, is practically freestanding and invites communication between the two levels. The saltbox form answered the demands of the site and the owner's preference for a modest house with a native New England character.

COKER

View of the living room showing the loft above the stairway.

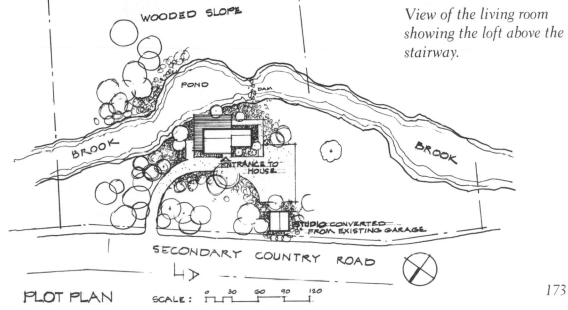

WOODED SLOPE

POND

DAM

BROOK

BROOK

ENTRANCE TO HOUSE

STUDIO CONVERTED FROM EXISTING GARAGE

SECONDARY COUNTRY ROAD

PLOT PLAN   SCALE: 0 30 60 90 120

FLOOR PLANS

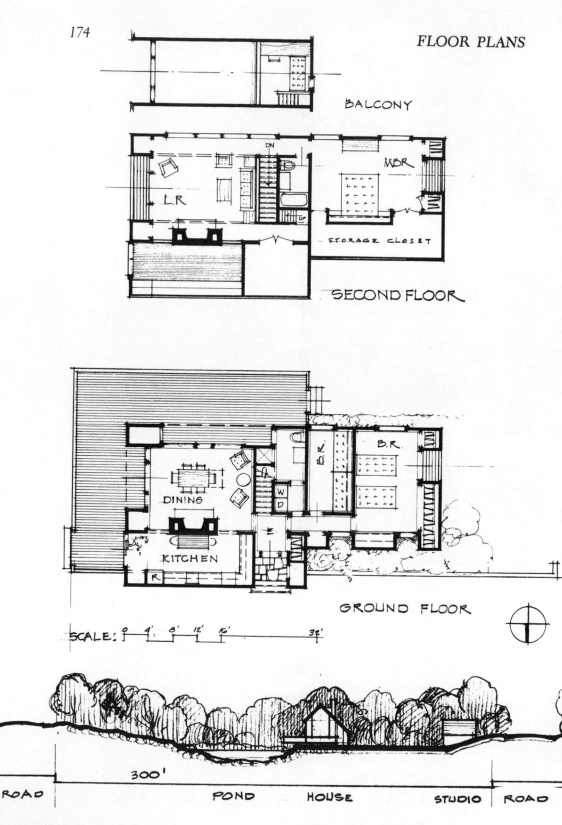

BALCONY

L.R

DN

MBR

STORAGE CLOSET

SECOND FLOOR

DINING

B.R.

B.R.

W
D

KITCHEN

R

GROUND FLOOR

SCALE: 0 4' 8' 12' 16'   32'

ROAD | 300' | POND | HOUSE | STUDIO | ROAD

SECTION A-A

Above: *The living room as first seen from the head of the stairs. The four-sided chimney mass is seen from all the major living spaces. Note the openings on each side of the masonry above and the view of the kitchen at the lower level (right).*

See also the pictures of the dining room on page 42.

View of the rear of the house from the southwest.

Willow Pond House was designed for a couple with two daughters in college. A romantic tower reminiscent of Ditta Coward's native Austria was part of the program.

The five-acre lot on the south side of a rural road featured a lovely pond with weeping willows. There was ample room to set the house well back from the road, providing a gracious approach, and to position the house so it commanded an advantageous view of the pond to the south.

The main approach.

The living room.

COWARD

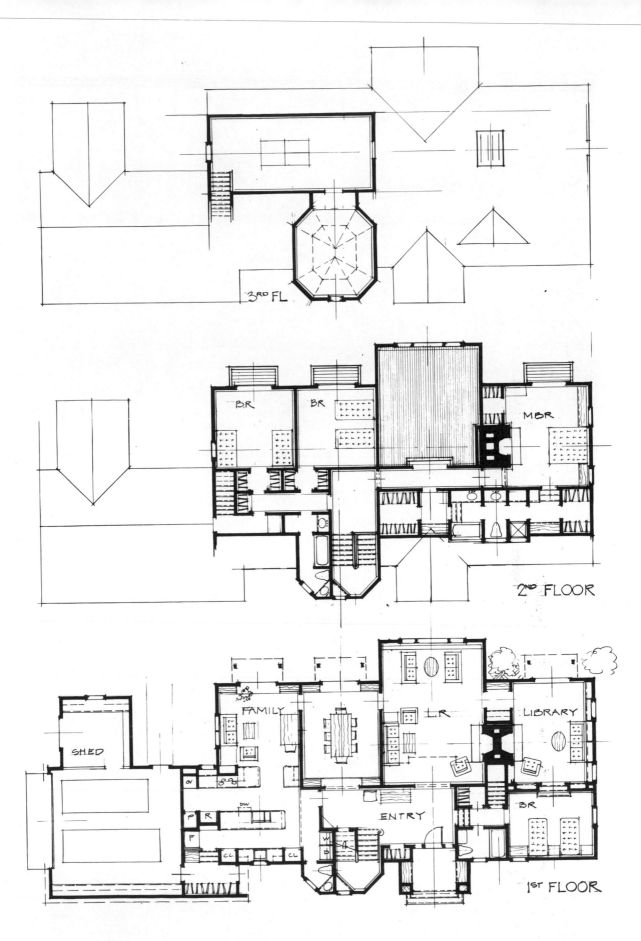

3RD FL

2ND FLOOR

BR   BR   MBR

1ST FLOOR

SHED

FAMILY   L.R   LIBRARY

OV

P R

DW

F

CL   CL

ENTRY

BR

The Marbury-Hansen house is a weekend retreat in a wooded area of Connecticut. The owners are avid gardeners and collectors of fine antique furniture and Oriental rugs, as well as modern prints and objets d'art. Though more open than their former seventeenth-century house across the road, the new house they built is more inward looking than most contemporary houses, reflecting the personal preference of the owners and showing that a contemporary house doesn't have to be all glass, chrome, and plastic. The enclosed garden around the pool, lacing together the main house and the poolhouse, creates a cohesive order to the complex of volumes.

Above: *View of front entrance*

Below: *Garden terrace across the pool*

MARBURY-HANSEN

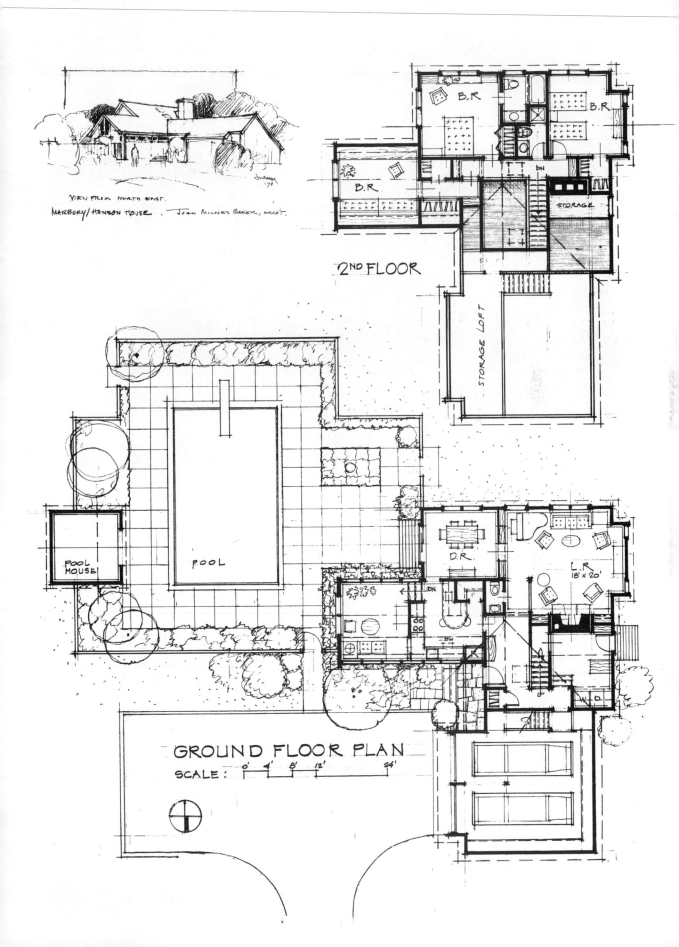

VIEW FROM NORTH EAST.

MARBURY/HANSON HOUSE . JOHN MILNES BAKER, ARCH'T.

2ND FLOOR

B.R

B.R

B.R

STORAGE

DN

STORAGE LOFT

POOL HOUSE

POOL

D.R.

L.R
18' X 20'

DN

BW

W.D

GROUND FLOOR PLAN

SCALE: 0' 4' 8' 12' 24'

Above: *The first view of the house, showing the inviting walkway that provides access to the elevated entrance.*

Below: *View from the dining area, looking toward the living-room fireplace. Note the entry door beyond and the opening at the master bedroom at the upper right.*

This beach house on New York's Fire Island was designed for a couple with grown children. It is basically a summer house, but the fireplace is used in the spring and fall.

It is oriented to capture the southwest breezes and a view of the ocean from the master bedroom on the upper floor.

The house is raised almost a full story above the ten-foot-wide walkway, the only road in the community, providing privacy in front and seclusion around the pool at the rear.

SILVER

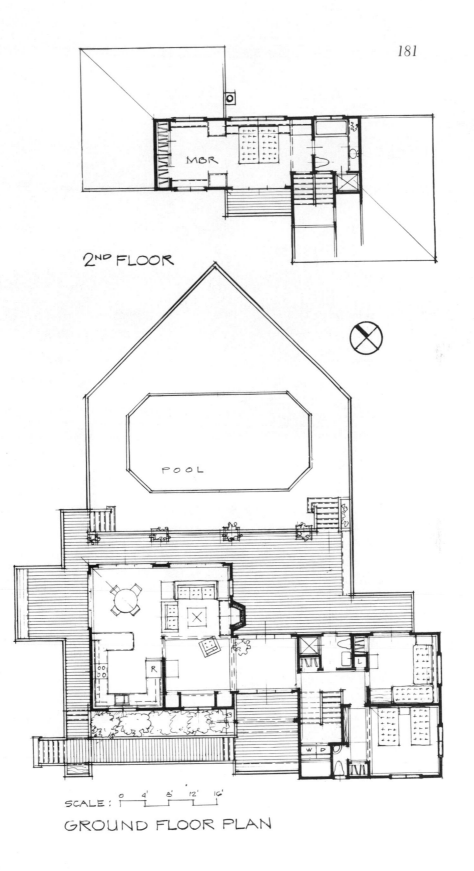

2ND FLOOR

POOL

MBR

R

L

W D

SCALE : 0 4' 8' 12' 16'

GROUND FLOOR PLAN

Above: *The back of the deck, looking across the pool.*

Left: *The master bathroom.*

Opposite: *View of the living room, dining room, and kitchen. Note that all sloped roofs have cathedral ceilings within.*

The Bents' beach house straddles a dune ridge which parallels the ocean on the south and a large bay to the north. With the main living space on the upper floor, all the major rooms enjoy extensive views in both directions.

The club community mandates shingle siding in keeping with the existing houses and encourages buildings that reflect the character of the older houses, which date back to the early 1900s. Respect for local character is an important design consideration.

(See the other houses in this community, pages 18 and 19.)

Above: *The house is first seen from an eight-foot-wide path limited to pedestrians and bicycles. Colorful wagons proliferate in this community, but there are no cars.*

BENT

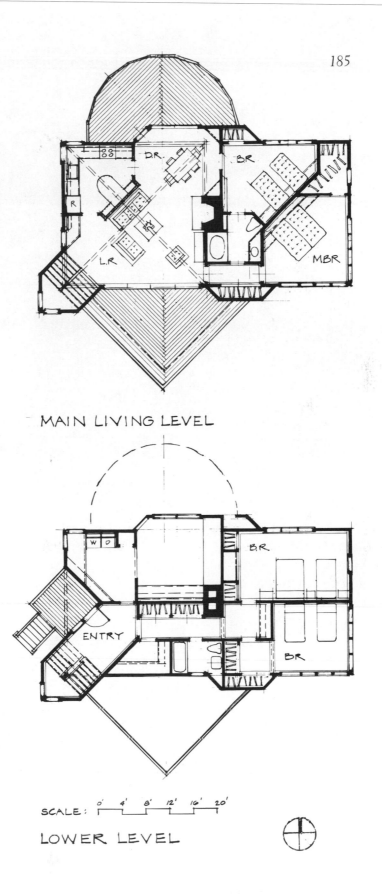

MAIN LIVING LEVEL

SCALE: 0' 4' 8' 12' 16' 20'

LOWER LEVEL

Above: *View of the house from the northwest—looking toward the entrance.*

Below: *The rocky ledge on the south is in sharp contrast to the level ground on the north.*

Tower Ledge was built as a vacation house in New York's Catskill Mountains for a family with grown children. The site enjoys magnificent views of the valley to the south, with more mountains beyond.

Three bedrooms plus a tower retreat met the original needs of the family. Seven years later, however, the house was enlarged to accommodate now married children and grandchildren.

BUCKNALL (ORIGINAL)

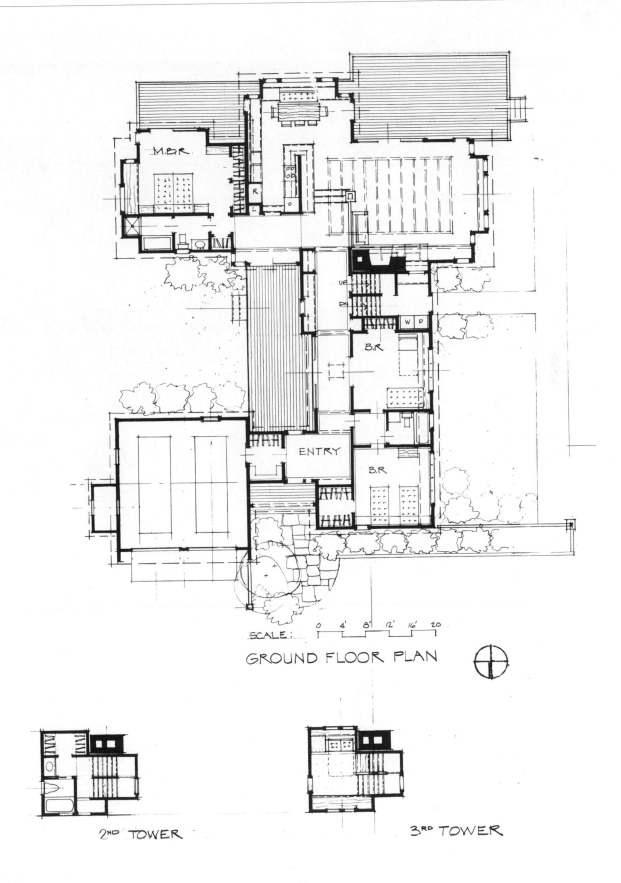

M.BR

ENTRY

B.R

B.R

SCALE :　0　4'　8'　12'　16'　20

GROUND FLOOR PLAN

2ND TOWER

3RD TOWER

Above: *View of living room from top of steps.*

Left: *Looking through kitchen toward dining area.*

Above: *View of fireplace wall of
living room as seen from dining
area.*

Right: *Looking toward the kitchen
and dining area from the northwest
corner of the living room.*

Above: *View of the enlarged house. The addition can be seen to the right and the original part with the tower on the left.*

Below: *A view of the new guest sitting room, which can double as a bedroom in a pinch.*

Married children with growing families required an expanded house. Note the enlargement of the original garage wing and its conversion to a guest sitting room, a back entry, a kitchenette, a bathroom, and an extra bedroom in the link to the new garage. There are also two extra bunk rooms—one next to the bath and the other in a "crow's nest" above the bath with ladder access next to the kitchenette.

BUCKNALL (ENLARGED)

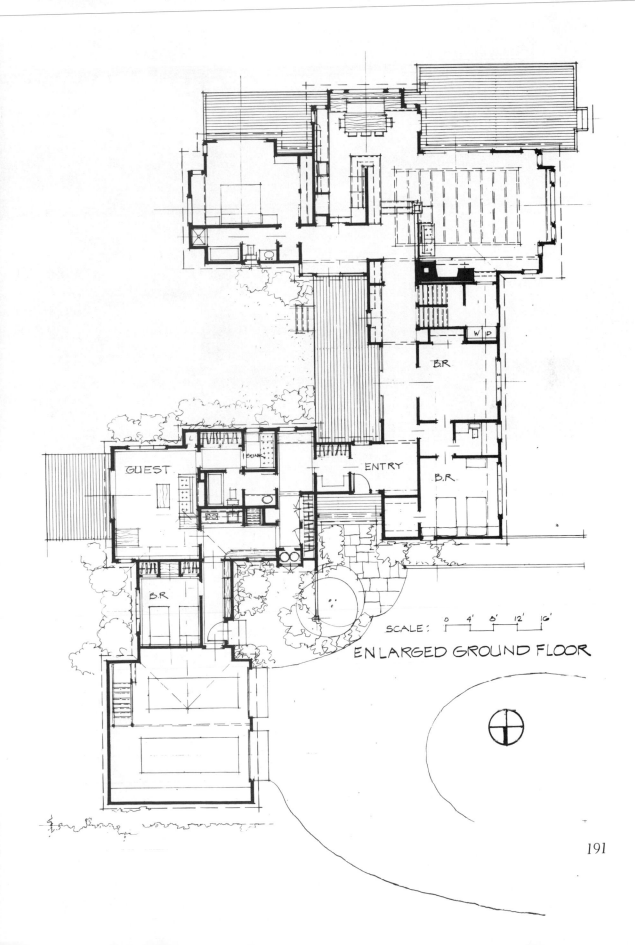

GUEST

BUNK

ENTRY

B.R

B.R

B.R

W D

SCALE: 0 4' 8' 12' 16'

ENLARGED GROUND FLOOR

191

Above: *View of the front, showing the house just over the edge of the embankment.*

Below: *The two-story facade on the downhill side.*

This 2,000-square-foot weekend house appears at first to be a cottage half that size. By being built just off the top of a sloped bank, the lower level is fully above the grade on the downhill side. The entrance bridge crosses a grassy "moat" and creates an interesting approach to the recessed entryway.

TUCKERMAN

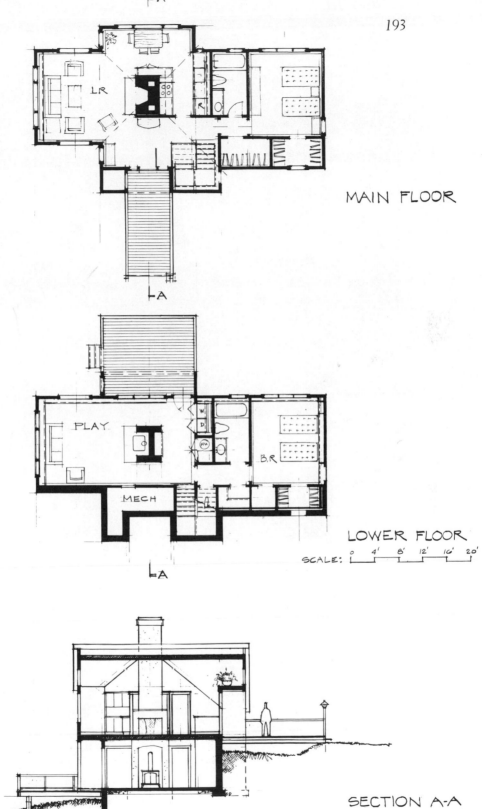

193

MAIN FLOOR

LR

LOWER FLOOR

SCALE: 0 4' 8' 12' 16' 20'

PLAY

MECH

B.R

SECTION A-A

Above: *View of the dining area from the opposite corner of the living room. The kitchen is tucked around the corner behind the chimney mass. (See right.)*

Above: *Looking across the
living room toward the front
door. The lowered ceiling at the
entryway creates a shelf space
with a half-round window
above. The change in ceiling
height just before entering adds
to the drama of the cathedral
ceilings of the interior.*

Right: *The chimney mass acts
as a pivotal divider between
the entry, the living room, the
dining area, and the kitchen.*

This house is currently under construction on lake-front property in the Litchfield Hills of Connecticut. The excitement of seeing a house being built cannot be captured in photographs, but it can perhaps be suggested as the volumes grow from a crisp and well-ordered floor plan.

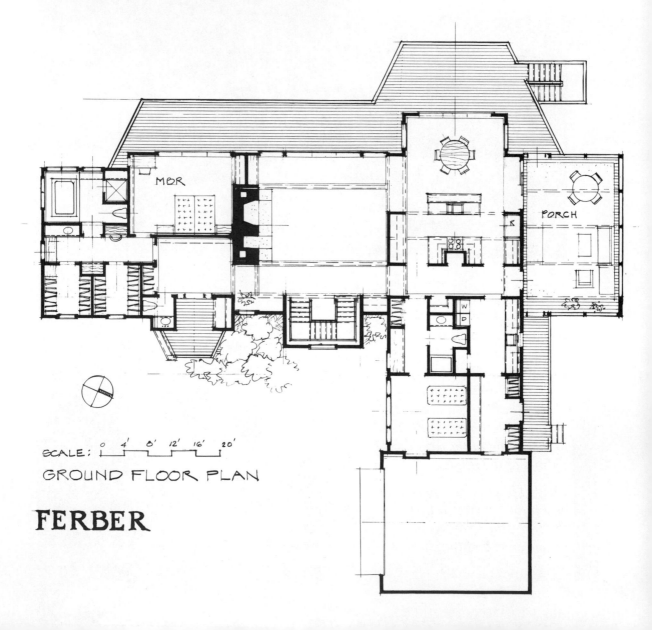

MBR

PORCH

SCALE: 0 4' 8' 12' 16' 20'

GROUND FLOOR PLAN

FERBER

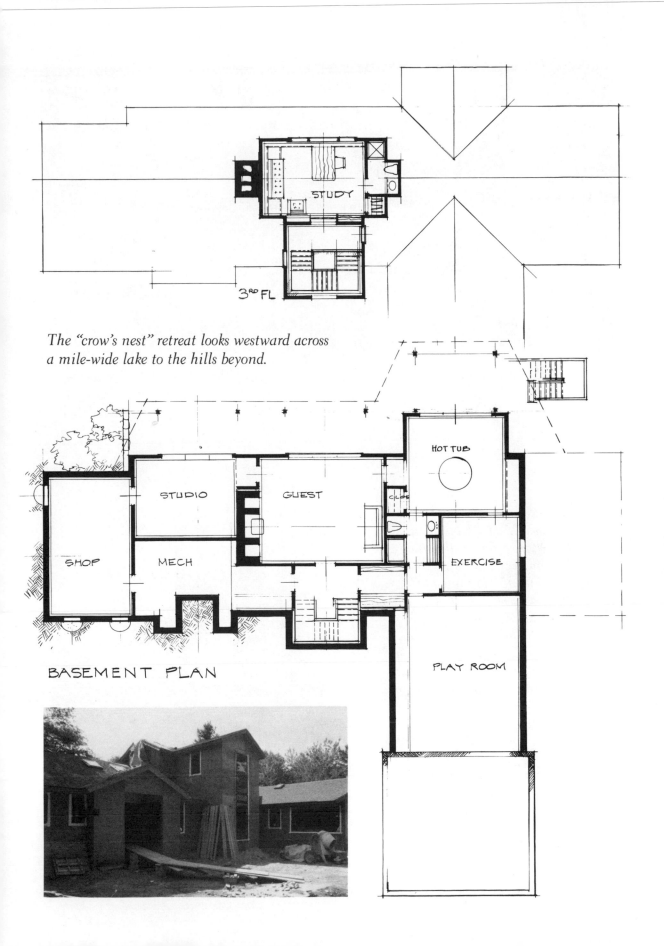

STUDY

3ᴿᴰ FL

*The "crow's nest" retreat looks westward across
a mile-wide lake to the hills beyond.*

HOT TUB

STUDIO

GUEST

CLOS

SHOP

MECH

EXERCISE

PLAY ROOM

BASEMENT PLAN

This house was designed for a wooded site in northern Westchester, with tall trees and existing stone walls which helped determine the building location. The two-and-a-half-story modified saltbox offers a variety of spaces, designed for specific purposes and special for each child's room. It is an eclectic house in many ways, but so are we as a family, and it responds to our needs. It was fun to plan and build, and we may even finish it someday, but certainly haven't yet. Welcome to the "elfin refuge of the Middle Earth." *

* Tolkien

The author's own house

RIVENDELL

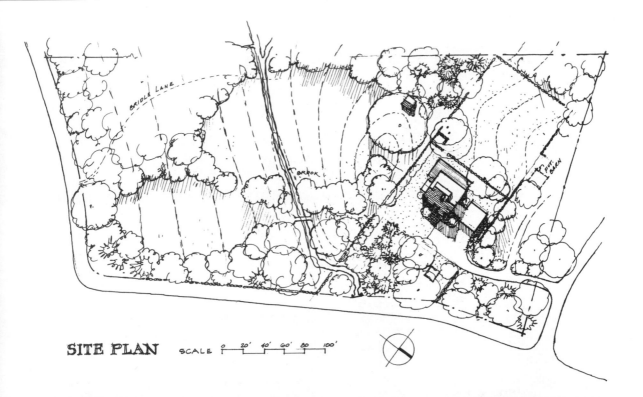

SITE PLAN   SCALE [0 20' 40' 60' 80' 100']

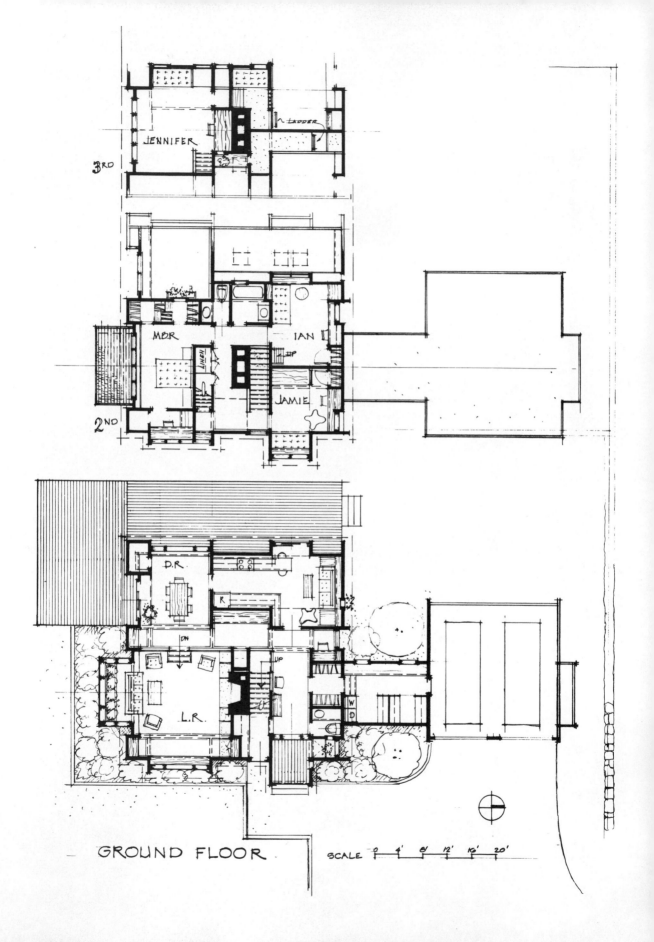

GROUND FLOOR   SCALE 0 4' 6' 12' 16' 20'

Above: *View approaching the living room. The dining room is around the corner to the right. (See also pages 43, 48, 52, 79, and 96 [bottom].)*

Right: *View of the kitchen, looking toward the sitting area.*

202

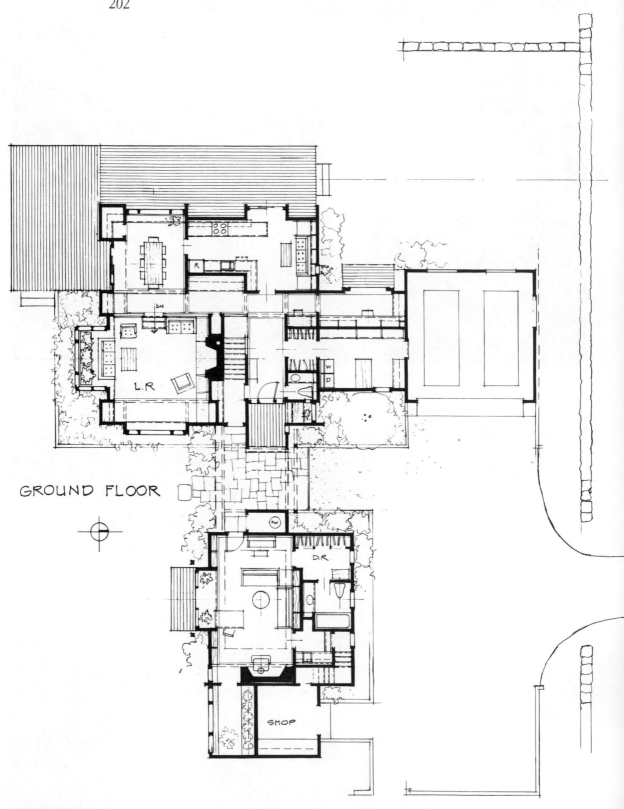

GROUND FLOOR

L.R

DN

R

W
D

RW

D.R

SHOP

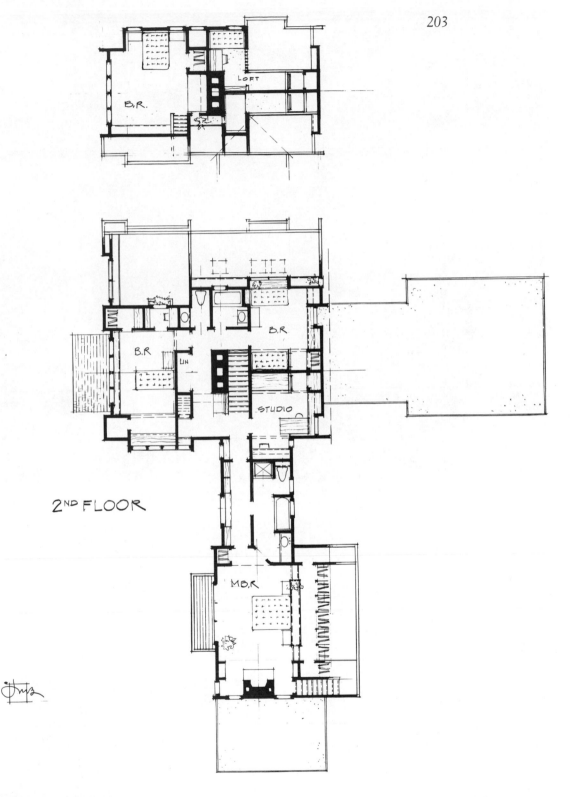

2ND FLOOR

RIVENDELL   GIRDLE RIDGE ROAD, KATONAH, NEW YORK

The south side of the author's house, showing the new addition at the right. Note the renderings on page 89 drawn over a decade before, when the house was first designed. The greenhouse moved to the right and a balcony replaced the second-floor window in the master bedroom. (It's also interesting to compare the rendering of the entrance side with the photograph on page 48.)

Right: *The office/library/guest room on the lower floor.*

The master bedroom.

View of the book-lined hallway that connects the original house with the new master bedroom on the upper level of the new wing.

The author's studio/office.

APPENDIX: THE ARCHITECT'S FEE

THE ARCHITECT'S FEE

For basic architectural services on a typical house costing about $200,000, you should expect to pay approximately 10 to 15 percent of the total cost of construction, and about 15 to 20 percent for alterations. The rate generally decreases somewhat as the cost of the work increases.

The architect's fee is usually a relatively insignificant part of the cost of the entire building project, including the actual construction cost (on which the architect's fee is computed), the furnishings and equipment, and the interest paid on the mortgage.

If you consider the cost of a house over a twenty-five-year period, your actual expenditure is probably two and a half times the initial price tag. Here is a somewhat simplified hypothetical case:

Land purchase price	$100,000
House construction cost	200,000
Architect's fee @ 12 percent of construction cost	24,000
Miscellaneous:	
broker's fee, closing costs, title insurance, etc.	10,000
Landscaping, driveway, etc.	12,000
Interest on $150,000 mortgage @ 11 percent	441,054
Taxes @ $4,000 per annum for 25 years	100,000
TOTAL	$887,054

The architect's fee, which is a once-and-for-all expense, is actually close to 5 percent of the cost of the house over a twenty-five-year period—not counting maintenance costs over the years, which would reduce the architect's percentage even more. This is a somewhat conservative example, because the mortgage is only 50 percent. A 75-percent mortgage in the same package would increase the interest considerably, and the architect's percentage, overall, would be reduced to around 4 percent. It is also worth noting that, even with a tight set of plans and specs, the range of prices in competitive bidding often varies by more than the amount of the architect's fee.

PAYMENTS FOR BASIC SERVICES

An initial retainer payment of 5 percent of the estimated fee is generally due upon the execution of the owner/architect agreement and is credited to the owner's account. The architect has shown his good faith by meeting with you; he has probably visited the site and gotten a "feel" for the scope and feasibility of the project.

Subsequent payments for so-called basic services are made monthly in proportion to services performed, so that the amount billed at the completion of each phase equals the following percentages of the fee:

Phase	Percent of Fee	
Schematic Design (Schematics)	15	15
Design Development (Preliminaries)	20	35
Construction Document (Working Drawings and Specifications)	40	75
Bidding or Negotiation	5	80
Construction	20	100

Whatever the payment schedule for the fee, monthly payments are made for reimbursable expenses. These include blueprints, toll calls made in the interest of the project, and the architect's out-of-pocket travel expenses, if the job is located at a distance. Usually a set amount per trip is established, depending upon the distance and whether any tolls are involved.

In the event that the scope of the work can be determined in advance and a fixed fee agreed upon, equal monthly payments can be established. For example, if the entire process takes a year and, by co-incidence, the fee is $24,000, the cash flow can be arranged on the basis of twelve incremental payments. Some months the architect will be ahead, some months you will be, but the simplicity of the arrangement makes it appealing to many clients and architects.

Under certain circumstances an inordinate amount of time may be spent on the schematic and developed design phases. For instance, the architect may have to explore an unconventional and innovative structural system, or a solution using solar heating or some other unusual feature. This extra time may well result in a lower building cost, but it will also produce a disproportionately low rate of payment per hour for the architect. In such an instance, it might be advisable to have the initial phases billed on a time basis, or per diem. The working drawings and construction phases could then be covered by a fixed fee, or they may be treated as direct personnel expenses. The American Institute of Architects defines direct personnel expenses as ". . . the salaries of professional, technical, and clerical employees engaged on the Project by the Architect and the cost of their mandatory and customary benefits such as statutory employee benefits, insurance, sick leave, holidays, vacations, pensions, and similar benefits."

There are several methods of compensation outlined in A.I.A. pamphlets. The two most commonly used in residential work are a percentage of construction cost and a fixed fee. Sometimes a professional fee plus expenses is used, but this is just a variation on the fixed-fee concept. Traditionally, the percentage of construction-cost method has been the most common. This allocates roughly one-third of the fee (for example, 5 percent of the construction cost in the case of a typical 15-percent fee) to basic design and feasibility studies; another third, or 5 percent, for working drawings and specifications; and the final third for the contractual and construction phase of the work. It is always a pay-as-you-go proposition.

One drawback to this method is that you may suffer from a nagging suspicion that the architect is deliberately raising the cost of the work so as to increase his fee. Though this would be highly unprofessional and is most unlikely, the thought can be there, and a fixed fee, independent of minor fluctuations in costs, is a more comfortable arrangement. A fixed fee, however, is only fair when the scope of the program and services is clearly defined.

When the percentage of construction-cost method is used, the fee is based on the "total cost or estimated cost to the Owner of all work designed or specified by the Architect." It does not normally include landscaping, the driveway, appliances, or anything you could take with you when you move.

PAYMENTS FOR ADDITIONAL SERVICES

There are, of course, numerous services that the architect provides in addition to the basic services that have been described in this book. These services are enumerated in "Standard Form of Agreement between Owner and Architect" (A.I.A. Document B141), but the following is a summary of those most pertinent to residential work:

Feasibility Studies

This includes an analysis of the owner's needs in the form of a preliminary program, a financial analysis, and perhaps an evaluation of one or more prospective sites. In the event that this work leads directly to an actual project, some portion of this fee could be applied toward the fee for subsequent work.

Future Work

Design services relating to projected work that is not intended as a part of the present project—future additions and expansions, for example—are in this category. If preliminaries are sufficient for the purpose, 5 percent of the projected cost is appropriate. If working drawings are required, another 5 percent of the estimated cost of the work is due, but the fee for the construction phase is deferred until the work is actually done.

Alternatives ("Alternates")

You may ask your architect to explore different options and provide documents for alternative bids. If only budget estimates are required at the schematic design phase, the architect normally does not charge an extra fee for such services. In the event that detailed drawings for both alternatives are necessary, however, the architect's fee would be the same as for future work.

Interior Design

These are services required for, or in connection with, the selection of furnishings and furniture. Usually an architect tries to be very accommodating to appreciative clients who seek his advice (and even his discount) in furnishing their new house. Certainly there is a fine line in residential work as to where the architect leaves off and the interior designer takes over. And it is undoubtedly in the architect's interest to see "his" house completed as thoroughly and as beautifully as possible. But it is not advisable to take advantage of an architect's good nature to such an extent that he begins to feel imposed upon. Remember, his interest in your house, though personal and cordial, is basically a professional one.

The architect's fee for interior design is best established on a per diem or an hourly rate; it will probably not be less than a couple of hundred dollars per day for concentrated consultation.

Revisions and Changes

If revisions of the contract documents are required because of additions or deletions you have made, the architect's fee must be adjusted. In the case of an "extra," 15 percent of the contractor's additional charge is usually agreeable to both the architect and the client. Sometimes it is preferable for the architect to charge for the work at an hourly rate or on a per diem basis.

If work is deleted for any reason after construction documents have been prepared, the architect's fee is naturally not reduced. Whatever time is involved in his effecting the change either comes within his regular fee or is billed on a time basis.

Problem Contractor

If the architect's work is increased because of the default of the contractor, major defects in his work, or even an extended delay beyond the projected completion date, the architect's remuneration should be increased. This amount should be entered in the owner/contractor agreement, and it is sometimes deducted from the final payment to the contractor.

Anyone contemplating engaging an architect should obtain a copy of the "Standard Form of Agreement between Owner and Architect" (A.I.A. Document B141 or B151). The document "... has important legal consequences ... (and) consultation with an attorney is encouraged with respect to its completion or modification." This document is available from any architect, the local chapter of the American Institute of Architects, or the national A.I.A. office at 1735 New York Avenue, N.W., Washington, D.C. 20006.

Let me emphasize once again: read the General Conditions of this document carefully; do the same with the contract, and raise any questions you may have with your architect *before* signing. It is far better to air any doubts you may have ahead of time than to face an unpleasant situation later on.

Glossary

A.I.A. The American Institute of Architects (1735 New York Avenue, N.W., Washington, D.C. 20006).

Air conditioning. *See* H.V.A.C.

Architect. A legal term referring to a professional licensed by one or more states to practice architecture. Even a graduate architect cannot use the appellative until he is registered.

Architectural designer. An unlicensed nonprofessional who designs buildings.

Backfill. A verb meaning to fill in an excavated trench or hole. The material used is also called backfill if it originally came out of the excavated area.

Bay. The distance or span between two principal column lines.

Beam. A horizontal supporting member.

Bearing wall. A wall that supports part of the structure above it.

Berm. An earth embankment placed against a masonry wall.

Blueprint. A full-size reproduction of a tracing-paper drawing. Originally white-line drawing on blue paper, but now generally any blue-line or black-line architectural print on white paper.

Bridging. Diagonal cross braces between joists that distribute floor loads to adjacent joists and generally stiffen the structure. "Solid bridging" is a rectangular stiffener placed between joists—usually the same dimension as the joists.

BUCK. A metal door frame.

CANTILEVER. A projecting or overhanging beam, slab, or portion of a building.

CASEMENT WINDOWS. Windows hinged on either side which swing in or out (usually out).

CASING. The trim surrounding a door, window, or other framed opening which is secured to both the jamb and the wall.

CAT. Reinforcing or blocking between joists, studs, or rafters to assure a solid backing for nails or screws.

CEMENT. A powder of calcined (burnt) rock or stone used to make concrete.

CONCRETE. A mixture of cement, water, sand, and stones (called aggregate) which hardens to a stonelike consistency.

CONTEMPORARY. Any modern house that does not derive its inherent character from traditional or derivative stylistic expressions, but from the nature of its own materials and structure.

CONVECTOR. A heating device which induces convection currents of air. Cool air is admitted at the bottom of an enclosure, heated as it passes over an element, and rises through an opening at the top. Baseboard radiation is not from radiators but from linear convectors.

DECK. Any wooden platform, porch, or horizontal surface. Sometimes refers to the plywood subfloor or flat roof of a house.

DUCT. A shaft, usually metal, used to transmit air for heating or cooling.

ELEVATION. Either a height above sea level or the interior or exterior walls of a house drawn to a given scale.

ENTOURAGE. An indication of planting on a floor plan, rendered elevation, or perspective drawing.

FASCIA. The finish board which covers the ends of roof rafters.

FENESTRATION. The window openings of a building. Often includes door openings as well.

FILL. Material used to fill a hole, trench, or depression. Usually implies material brought to the location from somewhere else (as opposed to the excavated material which is called backfill).

FINISH HARDWARE. Hardware, such as locks, hinges, and knobs, which you see when the house is finished (as opposed to straps, hangers, and clips used for structural purposes).

FIVE-QUARTER. Colloquial term meaning a board cut to 1¼ inches thick (and dressed to 1⅛ inches).

FLASHING. Metal used in such a way as to keep rain from entering a building at vulnerable cracks and joints.

FLOORING. Finish flooring material (as opposed to subflooring or underlayment).

FOOTING. Poured concrete base upon which the foundation walls, chimney, or columns rest.

FURRING. Wooden framework or strips used to thicken a wall or ceiling.

GIRDER. A horizontal beam carrying one or more intermediate beams.

GRADE. The slope of the ground with respect to a given reference point—usually the top of the foundation or the ground-floor elevation.

GYPSUM BOARD. Paper-based plaster wallboard panels usually ⅜ inch, ½ inch, or ⅝ of an inch thick. Often called by U.S. Gypsum Company's trade name: Sheetrock.

HEAD. Top section of a window, door, or other opening.

HEADER. A wooden beam in a floor or roof placed between two long beams and supporting the ends of one or more intermediate beams or tailpieces.

HIP. The sloping ridge formed by the intersection of two adjacent roof planes.

HOME. An occupied primary residence or dwelling place.

HOUSE. A building constructed as a residence or dwelling.

H.V.A.C. Heating, ventilating, air conditioning, and cooling. (Air conditioning means cleaning, humidifying, dehumidifying, and filtering of air—not just cooling.)

JAMB. The sides of a door or window opening.

JOIST. Horizontal framing beams of a floor or ceiling.

LALLY COLUMN. Concrete-filled pipe column.

LEFT-HAND DOOR. A door which opens toward you when the knob is to your left and away from you when the knob is to your right.

LIGHT (WINDOW). A window light is a pane of glass (sometimes refers to a whole sash as in skylight.)

LINTEL. A load-bearing beam which spans a door or window opening.

LIVE LOAD. The variable weight imposed upon a building by people, furniture, and equipment.

MILLWORK. Any wooden component part of a structure which is made in a wood-working shop or factory and installed in a building.

MODERN. A house built with twentieth-century skills and materials. Usually means contemporary but could be a modern reproduction.

MODERNISTIC. A derogatory term for a copy or imitation contemporary.

MULLION. A vertical post, frame, or double jamb dividing two window sashes or large panes of fixed glass.

MUNTIN. The crosspieces dividing the panes of glass within a window sash.

N.C.A.R.B. National Council of Architectural Registration Boards.

N.I.C. Not-in-contract. Used in plans or specs to indicate an item not included in the price agreed upon in the original contract.

NOSING. Projecting edge of a molding or overhanging edge of a stair tread.

OWNER. A person (or group) who owns the land on which a house is to be built.

PARTI (pronounced "par-tee"). The architect's resolution of a design concept.

PARTITION. A wall or partial wall which divides two spaces.

PLAN. A drawing or a diagram, usually drawn to scale, showing either the arrangement of the rooms of a house or a horizontal section of a detail.

PLATE. The horizontal framing member at the top of a wall.

PLENUM. An air space or chamber used in an air-conditioning system.

POCHÉ. The darkening of the structural members or walls of a floor plan or cross section—either black, colored, or cross-hatched.

PRINTS. Copies of tracing-paper drawings. *See also* BLUEPRINT.

R.A. Registered architect. A person licensed to practice architecture.

RABBET. A continuous notch or cut in the corner of a board or timber.

RADIANT HEAT. Usually used in architecture for heat derived from hot water or steam pipes placed in a concrete floor slab. (Frank Lloyd Wright called it "gravity heat," a more accurate term sometimes used instead of "radiant heat" for that type of heating. Ceiling or wall panels with electrical elements are actually a source of radiant heat.)

RADIATOR. A heating device which "radiates" heat—most commonly a series of hollow cast-iron sections through which hot water or steam is forced.

RAFTER. Sloping roof beam.

RAKE. The slope or pitch of the gable end of a roof or rafter.

RENDERING. A pictorial representation or perspective of a building or some aspect of it.

RETAINING WALL. A vertical masonry wall used to hold back earth.

REVEAL. Side wall next to a recessed door or window.

RIDGE. The horizontal line formed by the juncture of two sloping ʀoofs.

RIDGEPOLE. The horizontal beam at the ridge of a roof to which the rafters are secured. (Also called a ridge beam or ridge piece.)

RIGHT-HAND DOOR. A door which opens toward you when the knob is on the right and away from you when the knob is on the left.

RISER. The vertical distance between stair treads. The material used to fill that void is also called a riser. If the void is not filled at all, the stair is an "open-riser" stair.

ROUGHING. The basic plumbing, heating, and electrical work which eventually is hidden within the structure.

ROUGH OPENING. Distance between framing members.

SADDLE. A threshold of a door, a metal or wood or marble tread, usually not more than ⅝ of an inch high, the full width of the opening.

SASH. The part of a window in which the glass is set. It is the movable part of a window, though some sashes are fixed and do not operate.

SCALE. A reference standard in measurement. A device bearing the marks of a relative measurement. Proportion relating a representation of an object to what it represents. A calibrated line to indicate such a proportion.

SECTION. A view of an object or building from an imaginary plane cut vertically through an object. (A floor plan is actually a horizontal section, but it is never called that.)

SEPIA. A brownish transparent copy of a tracing-paper drawing which can be drawn on and from which prints can be made.

SHEATHING. Plywood, composition sheathing board, or 1-inch board nailed to frame of building as underlayer of wall.

SIDING. The outside "skin" of a building.

SILL. (a) Bottom section of a window or door; (b) wooden framing member bolted to the foundation.

SLEEPER. A furring strip placed on a subfloor.

SOFFIT. The underside of an architectural element, either a structural component or the bottom of an overhang.

STOP. A molding or battenlike strip against which a door or window "stops."

STUD. Two-by-four (usually) vertical framing member in a wood frame house.

TREAD. The horizontal surface of a stair.

TWO-BY-FOUR. A piece of lumber, originally cut to a full 2 inches by 4 inches, with finished dimensions of $1\frac{5}{8}$ inches by $3\frac{5}{8}$ inches.

UNDERLAYMENT. Plywood, Masonite, or particle board laid on top of a subfloor as the base for carpeting or resilient tile.

WET WALL. A wall with plumbing pipes in it.

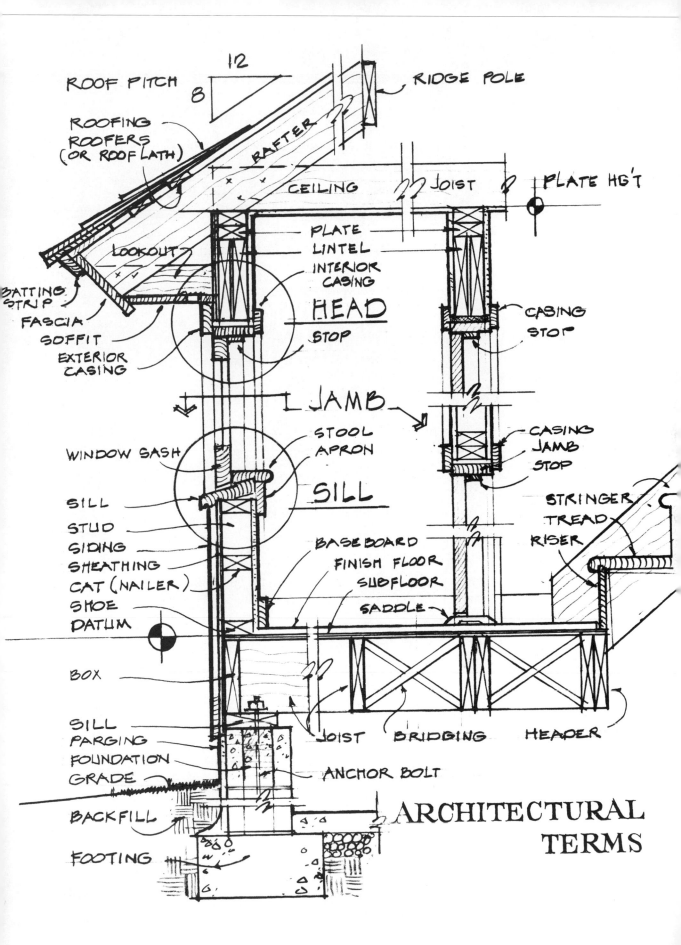

ROOF PITCH

ROOFING
ROOFERS
(OR ROOF LATH)

RIDGE POLE

RAFTER

CEILING   JOIST   PLATE HG'T

BATTING
STRIP
FASCIA
SOFFIT
EXTERIOR
CASING

LOOKOUT

PLATE
LINTEL
INTERIOR
CASING
HEAD
STOP

CASING
STOP

JAMB

CASING
JAMB
STOP

WINDOW SASH

STOOL
APRON
SILL

SILL
STUD
SIDING
SHEATHING
CAT (NAILER)
SHOE
DATUM

BASEBOARD
FINISH FLOOR
SUBFLOOR
SADDLE

STRINGER
TREAD
RISER

BOX

SILL
PARGING
FOUNDATION
GRADE

JOIST   BRIDGING   HEADER

ANCHOR BOLT

BACKFILL

FOOTING

ARCHITECTURAL
TERMS

Suggestions for Further Reading

Berg, Donald J. *How to Build a House in the Country*. Berkeley, Calif.: Ten Speed Press, 1986.

An excellent book with valuable suggestions, hints, and guidelines collected by the architect-author from nineteenth-century publications. Covers each phase of building. A delightful book with quotes that are incredibly timely and up-to-date.

Conran, Terence. *The House Book*. New York: Crown, 1976.

An extraordinarily attractive book full of home-decorating ideas, profusely illustrated with color photographs.

Faulkner, Sarah, and Faulkner, Ray. *Inside Today's Home*. New York: Holt, Rinehart & Winston, 1968.

An in-depth analysis of every aspect of residential design. A most valuable book.

Ireys, Alice Recknagel. *How to Plan and Plant Your Own Property*. New York: M. Barrows, 1967.

Ms. Ireys has a touch for landscape design that makes a studied solution appear to be a natural complement to the house.

Kennedy, Robert Woods. *The House and the Art of Its Design*. New York: Reinhold Publishing Co., 1953.

Though first published over 3½ decades ago, this is an extremely thorough book and still helpful to anyone building a house today.

Moore, Charles, Allen, Gerald, and Lyndon, Donlyn. *The Place of Houses*. New York: Holt, Rinehart & Winston, 1974.

An interesting and personal analysis of houses. The architect authors offer examples from their own files and include an extremely helpful checklist of things to consider in developing a program.

Orton, Vrest. *The Forgotten Art of Building a Good Fireplace*. Dublin, N.H.: Yankee, Inc., 1974.

A delightful account of the theories and dictums of Count Rumford (1753–1814), a New Hampshire Yankee who was fascinated by fireplaces. Don't build a fireplace before you read this book!

Raskin, Eugene. *Architecturally Speaking*. New York: Bloch Publishing Co., 1954 and 1966.

Clarifies twelve key abstract terms used in discussing architecture in a witty and amusing way.

Raskin, Eugene. *Architecture and People*. Englewood Cliffs, N.J.: Prentice-Hall, 1974.

An informative book based on Professor Raskin's lectures at Columbia University's School of Architecture. He offers insights into architects and the profession as well as the ethical, social, and economic aspects of the field.

Rybczynski, Withold. *Home: A Short History of an Idea*. New York: Viking Penguin Inc., 1986.

This intriguing book examines the history of the concept of "home"—the nature of such subjects as domesticity, comfort, and privacy and how it affects our notion of residential design.

Stoddard, Alexandra. *Style for Living: How to Make Where You Live You*. Garden City, N.Y.: Doubleday, 1974.

This book about interior design is written with sensitivity and personal charm.

Wright, Frank Lloyd. *The Natural House*. New York: Horizon Press, 1964.

Wright's philosophy of organic architecture expressed in terms of the Usonian House. A stimulating text for anyone thinking of building a house.

Copyright Acknowledgments

Tom Crane: pp. 18, 31, 32, 33, 35–38, 46, 53, 70, 87, 141–143, 158, 160–162, 164, 166, 167, 178, 199, 201.
Ben Schnall: pp. 42, 139, 172, 173, 175 (courtesy of *House Beautiful*).
Jennifer Dickenson: pp. 147, 190.
All others by the author.

DRAWINGS
Paul Coker, Jr.: p. 100.
All others by the author.